Hudson Valley Homicide

True stories of jealousy, greed, sex, and insanity,
including serial killers and
a forgotten mass murderer.

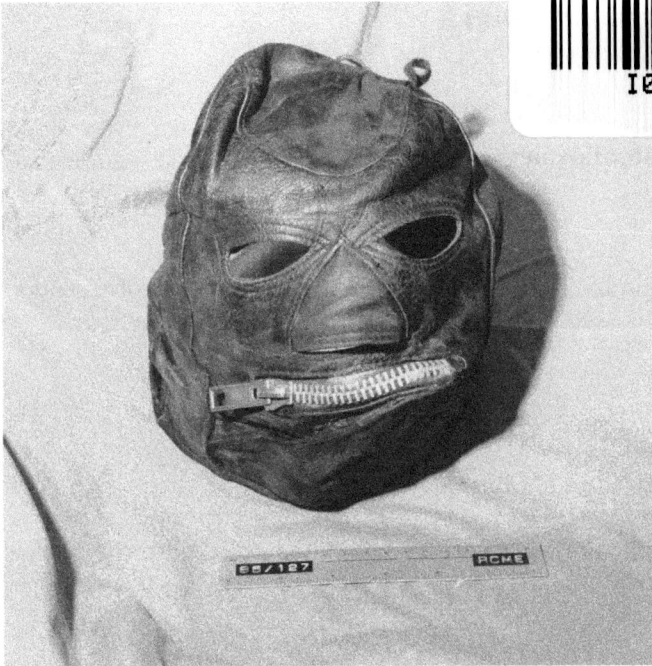

Written by
Linda Zimmermann

Eagle Press, New York

Linda Zimmermann's Facebook Fan Page

http://www.facebook.com/pages/Linda-Zimmermann/116636310250

Questions, comments, new cases, photos, or evidence to share?

Write to:

Linda Zimmermann
P.O. Box 192
Blooming Grove, NY 10914

Or send email to:

lindazim@optonline.net

What else is Linda Zimmermann writing? Go to: **www.gotozim.com**

Hudson Valley Homicide

Copyright © 2018 Linda Zimmermann

All rights reserved. This book may not be reproduced in whole or in part without permission.

Eagle Press, New York

ISBN: 978-1-937174-02-6

CONTENTS

Acknowledgements

What would I have done without Michael Worden's legal expertise to help me navigate through all the criminal charges, appeals, court decisions, and the tangled maze that is our justice system?

Many thanks to the law enforcement agencies who provided essential photos and information. Specifically, Hank Bender, BCI, Rockland County Sheriff's Office, John Davi, Columbia County Sheriff's Office, James Buckley, Bergen County Sheriff's Office, the Westchester County Office of the District Attorney (WCDA), and the Town of Poughkeepsie Police Department.

And my apologies to my husband, Bob Strong, who is now hooked on murder mysteries.

About the Author

Linda Zimmermann is a researcher, historian, lifelong resident of the Hudson Valley, and award-winning author of over 30 books. She has made numerous appearances on television and radio, and is intrigued by all things historic and mysterious.

Introduction

What do you get when you take the tranquil Hudson Valley and add four serial killers, a mass murderer, and a handful of other men and women with guns, knives, and axes, all who have homicidal tendencies?

You get a fascinating history of unthinkable criminal acts perpetrated against spouses, family members, and complete strangers in a region where still to this day, some people don't even lock their doors.

The cases in this book span over a century, and occur in quiet, rural areas, and in bustling town centers. These homicides were committed by both genders, and by people ranging in age from a teen to a senior citizen. The murderers were both highly educated and intelligent, as well as those who were most decidedly not either. In other words, there is no discernible pattern, no cookie cutter description of who is capable of committing these brutal crimes.

The next murderer or serial killer could be anyone; your boss, your neighbor, your brother, your best friend, or your wife.

Perhaps after reading this book, you'll make sure all of your doors are locked.

Linda Zimmermann
Hudson Valley
August 2018

Marriage in Pieces

Crime Scene

As residents of Celia Gardens apartments on Middletown Road in Pearl River, NY awoke on Easter Sunday, April 7, 1996, nothing seemed out of the ordinary. The downstairs neighbor of 49-year-old Dr. Yakov Gluzman—a famous cancer researcher at Lederle Labs just down the street—had heard some hammering or banging sounds between 2:30-3am, as if someone was moving furniture, but it wasn't enough to warrant a complaint to the police.

Celia Gardens in Pearl River.
Google Maps image.

Gluzman's apartment was quiet that morning because he was not there, which was odd, as he usually worked Saturday nights in the lab until 11:30pm, so he should have been home asleep. There were no signs of a forced entry, but there were some small bloodstains in the bathroom, on the walls and carpet in the apartment, and on the staircase leading downstairs, but certainly nothing that indicated to his neighbors that a serious crime had been committed, and the other residents had no reason to be suspicious of anything.

However, things did look suspicious that morning for East Rutherford, New Jersey Police Officer Richard Freeman as he sipped his coffee in his car overlooking the Passaic River. There were two cars by the river with their trunks open, a Ford Taurus and a Nissan Maxima, and

1

there was one man carrying two large, plastic garbage bags. The man went to the water's edge and dropped in one of the bags. Thinking that this was a simple case of illegal trash dumping, Officer Freeman approached the man, but quickly realized it wasn't so simple.

The man was wearing a bloody rubber glove, and there was also blood on his pants and shoes. And there was that distinctive "sickly sweet" smell in the air, a smell Freeman knew all too well was blood, and a lot of it. While kids across the country were eagerly hunting hidden Easter Eggs, the police made a far more gruesome discovery hidden in those plastic garbage bags—they were filled with pieces of a human body.

The body, which was later determined to be Dr. Gluzman, had been cut up into 65 pieces, and at first the coroner didn't even know how many victims there were! To try to avoid identification of all the bits of corpse, even the fingertips, nose, and lips had been cut off. The genitals had been sliced off, too. The bloody pieces of flesh and bone had been stuffed into nine *Hefty Steel-Sak* garbage bags. A tenth bag contained Yakov's clothing, along with the axes, hacksaw, and butcher knives used to kill and dismember him. All of the bags and pieces were recovered in the trunks of the two cars, and by divers in the river where the suspect was in the process of dumping them before he was interrupted.

Yakov Gluzman

The man disposing of the body was Vladimir Zelenin, a recent Russian émigré. Zelenin was the cousin and employee of 48-year-old Rita Gluzman, Yakov's wife, and he was literally caught red-handed, from both Yakov's blood, and from a nasty wound to his right hand.

Police subsequently were unable to locate Rita that morning, and many questions arose: Had Zelenin killed both the husband and wife? Zelenin could not have acted alone in this horrific crime as there were two cars at the scene, but who was his accomplice? Was Rita somehow involved? And above all, what possible motive could there have been to murder and butcher this renowned scientist?

The murder weapons and tools of dismemberment, still bloody and covered with bits of flesh. Note the tip of one of the butcher knives is broken, which Zelenin later explained occurred when he was cutting up the body.

Photo courtesy of the Bergen County Sheriff's Office.

Investigation

It is bizarre and disturbing how many murder cases begin with love stories, and the love story of Yakov and Rita Gluzman was something out of a Hollywood movie. Yakov was a Ukrainian student who had married his childhood friend, Rita, in 1969. As they were Jewish, they had requested that the Soviet Union allow them to emigrate to Israel. After repeated denials, in 1970, Rita, her son, and her parents were allowed to leave, but not Yakov.

3

Rita came to America and fought tirelessly for her husband's release. In 1971, she managed to meet with the United Nations Secretary-General U Thant and the U.S. Ambassador to the United Nations, George Bush. She went on an 18-day hunger strike in front of the U.N. which was covered extensively by the press. She protested every chance she got and she never gave up—until Yakov was finally released.

In Rita's words, "It was exactly like a dream," to be free, to leave the Soviet Union and have their family reunited and live the American Dream. So how did it all become a nightmare that ended in an ax murder 25 years later?

In custody, Zelenin told police what had happened in the months leading up to the savage crime. It was Rita who had come to him and asked for his help in murdering her once beloved husband. Rita had apparently embraced the American Dream a little too vigorously and demanded a large home on 24 Peach Tree Place in the very upscale town of Upper Saddle River, NJ. She burned through Yakov's six-figure salary from Lederle Labs every year buying clothes, furs, jewelry, and luxury cars. She also needed constant cash infusions to keep afloat her own company, ECI Technologies. Yakov finally had enough of Rita's extravagance and moved out in 1995 to his spartan, quiet, little apartment in Pearl River that was conveniently located just minutes from Lederle.

The expensive home on Peach Tree Place in Upper Saddle River, NJ
which Rita Gluzman complained was "a shack."

If that wasn't enough of a perceived insult to Rita, Yakov then filed for divorce, and had even fallen in love with a fellow scientist in Israel. He planned to move there to live with her and start a pharmaceutical company.

The divorce negotiations were bitter, with accusations flying back and forth. Rita demanded the settlement award her $6,212 a month, which included $1,000 a month for clothing, $860 for domestic help, and even $225 for pet care! And, she thought, if Yakov did move to Israel, ECI Technologies was sure to fail. After all she had done to fight for Yakov's release, this was how he was repaying her love and loyalty—or so it seemed in Rita's jealous, avaricious, hate-filled heart and soul.

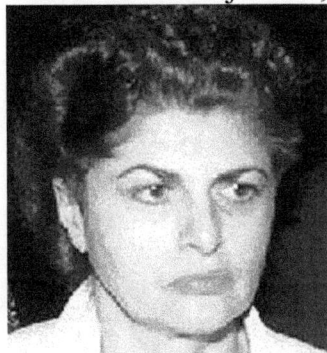

Rita Gluzman

Zelenin stated that he felt he was indebted to Rita for his coming to America, and afraid of losing his job at ECI, so on the night of April 6, he went with her to Yakov's apartment. Rita had previously sweet-talked Yakov into giving her a key, so they were easily able to enter with their murder kit of weapons and cleaning supplies. They knew Yakov was a creature of habit and would be home at 11:30pm, so they waited quietly in the dark—each holding an ax—for their unsuspecting victim.

According to Zelenin, "When Yakov came in, we jumped at him. I hit him with the ax to the head. I hit him twice. I cannot say whether it was simultaneous or who hit first."

Then Rita went into a murderous frenzy with her ax, repeatedly, brutally, and mercilessly striking her husband in the head and torso. In the midst of the bloodbath, she accidentally hit Zelenin and "'one of the blows went through my hand," he would later state, but that didn't stop her savage assault. Once she was finished with the ax, she took the large butcher knife and stabbed Yakov in the chest, just in case there was one breath of life left in him.

The deadly deed done, the cleanup and disposal began.

According to Zelenin, while Rita scrubbed the bloody crime scene in "stony silence," he dragged Yakov's body into the bathtub. Using a hacksaw, scalpel, and knives, he thoroughly dismembered the brilliant scientist into 65 pieces in hopes that there wouldn't be anything large enough to identify. Zelenin would later testify that after he finished cutting and hacking apart Rita's husband, he lit a cigarette in the kitchen. She flew

5

into a rage and yelled, "No smoking should be allowed here!" Apparently, atrocities were acceptable, but smoking crossed the line.

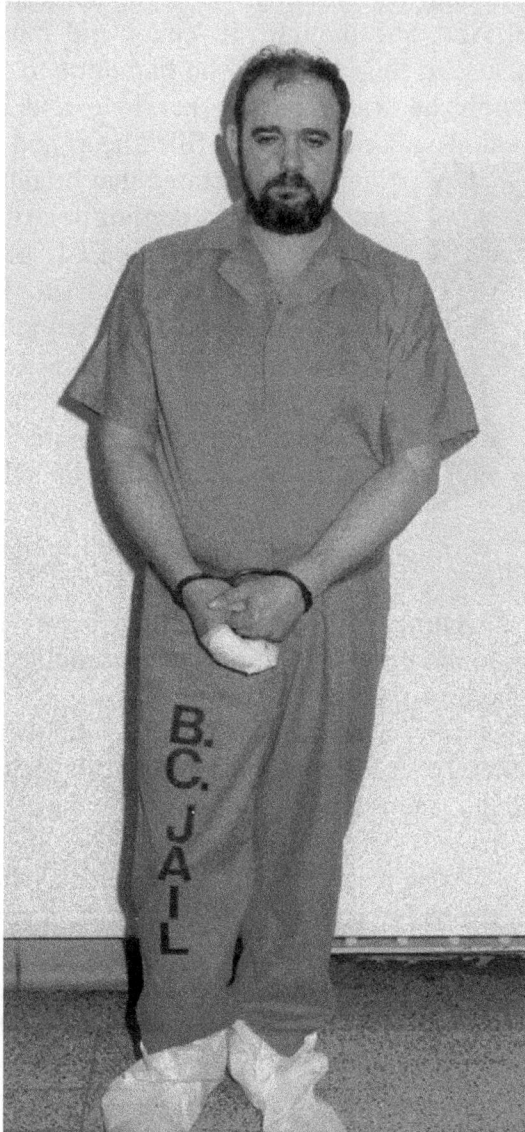

Vladimir Zelenin in the Bergen County, NJ jail. Note the bandage on his hand where Rita Gluzman had accidentally struck him with an ax during the murder.
Photo courtesy of the Bergen County Sheriff's Office.

The gruesome task complete, they filled the plastic bags with the all the pieces of the body, clothing, and instruments of death and dismemberment, and carried them down the staircase. They loaded the bags into the trunk of the Ford Taurus registered to Rita's company, ECI, and also into the trunk of Yakov's own car, the Nissan Maxima.

There was a moment of panic for the two butchers when the car alarm in the Taurus started going off, and Rita told Zelenin to drive away before the residents of Celia Gardens started looking out their windows to see what was happening. Fortunately for them, however, car alarms rarely elicited any kind of response back then as they were common occurrences, and it appeared that no one had noticed. After driving around for a while, Zelenin returned to finish the task.

Once all the bags were loaded, they drove the two cars to the Passaic River, about 30 miles away, but only a few hundred yards from ECI. Rita left Zelenin with the job of dumping the bags in the river, which was supposed to be done by daybreak. However, they were way behind schedule, as they had to stop at a CVS in Fair Lawn, NJ to get bandages for Zelenin's hand, and they underestimated the amount of time it took to cut up the body and clean up all the blood, so it was already 11am when Officer Freeman spotted Zelenin.

On Friday, April 12, the *Rockland Journal News* reported that as the crime had been committed in Pearl River, a Rockland County grand jury had indicted Zelenin on second-degree murder and District Attorney Michael Bongiorno would seek to have him extradited to Rockland. They knew Zelenin had an accomplice, but that was all they were telling the public.

"While investigators have refused to call Rita Gluzman a suspect," the article continued, "they are concerned she has fled the country, possibly to Israel or Russia. She has not returned to her Saddle River, N.J. home or been seen in the northern New Jersey area since Zelenin's arrest Sunday, police said."

Of course, within the police department, she was accomplice suspect number one, and the hunt was on for Rita Gluzman, but she was nowhere to be found. Police did know she was very much alive, however, as her cell phone records showed that since the murder she had been making numerous calls. With every passing minute, the risk of her leaving the country increased, so the clock was ticking.

Dismembered Body of Russian Scientist Found

EAST RUTHERFORD, N.J. (AP) — Hacked up body parts found in eight large garbage bags have been identified as those of a prominent Russian cancer researcher.

His estranged wife, ed a nationwide bulletin was being circulated among law enforcement agencies to be on the lookout for Mrs. Gluzman, 48, or the 1995 blue Ford Taurus she is believed to be driving

Newspapers across the country carried stories of the shocking details of the Gluzman murder, as far away as the *Daily Sitka Sentinel* in Alaska, 4/10/96.

At noon on April 12, time ran out for Rita Gluzman. Before taking the position at Lederle, Yakov worked at Cold Spring Harbor Laboratory in Long Island, NY. There were guest cottages on the property, one of which was supposed to be empty. As a housekeeper entered that cottage, she found a fire burning in the fireplace, four stolen license plates, travel brochures, and other items indicating that someone had been there—someone who had jumped out of a window and started running. Notifying security, they began looking for the mystery intruder.

The facility's dining hall was packed with scientists, and a woman with brightly-dyed, auburn hair and flashy clothes was trying to blend in, but was sticking out like a sore thumb, and security quickly apprehended the person who had trespassed and broken into the cottage. They could have just given her a warning and released her, or charged her with burglary and trespassing and released her, but someone on the staff recognized her as Rita Gluzman—and, he had heard on the radio that Yakov had been murdered and his wife was being sought for questioning.

Police now had Zelenin, Rita, the pieces of Yakov's body, the murder weapons, and evidence of the crime at Yakov's apartment. They also had Zelenin's confession and statement of Rita's involvement. Unfortunately, what they didn't have was any hard evidence that Rita had actually taken part in the crime, and under New York State law, they would need more than Zelenin's testimony for a conviction.

Knowing without a doubt that someone committed a crime is one thing, proving it in court was a totally different animal. Would Rita

Gluzman—whom the tabloids dubbed the Jewish Lizzie Borden—literally get away with murder?

Rita's family hired attorney Michael Rosen, a lawyer whose claim to fame was defending mobsters like the Gambino crime family. Rosen knew that it would be difficult to make murder charges stick without direct evidence against Rita—which the police did not have at the time—so after a judge initially rejected bail for Rita, Rosen filed for "Felony Examination," which essentially gave police and prosecutors 48 hours to produce some compelling evidence, or let his client go.

After only two days in jail and no evidence to put Rita at the murder scene, or put a weapon in her hand, she was released from the Nassau County Jail on $250,000 bail. Rosen knew there would still likely be serious charges to deal with, possibly accessory to murder, but that's what he did for living—he got criminals out of trouble. In an interview, Rosen even once stated, "I'll never forget this as long as I live. I was on the FDR Drive, coming home, flushed with victory after having gotten her bail. I'm expecting her to be in the arms of her family."

How lawyers can be so proud of themselves—"flushed with victory"—for letting someone like a brutal ax murderer out of jail is beyond the comprehension of decent people, but fortunately, prosecutors in Rockland had some tricks up their sleeves, as well.

Knowing they most likely would never have enough evidence to fulfill the burden of proof to convict Rita of murder, they found a legal ace in the hole. A federal law had been passed as part of the Violence Against Women Act of 1994, which basically mandated harsh punishments for a person who crossed state lines to injure his or her spouse, especially if those injuries led to death. Of course, the law was designed to protect battered wives, and had yet to be used against a woman, or for a homicide, but this case fit the letter of the law. They couldn't let Rita walk, so it was well worth trying.

In the midst of Rosen's euphoria on his drive home, he was suddenly bitterly disappointed when he got the call that new charges were being filed against his client and he needed to turn around and head back to Nassau County.

Feds: Wife was mastermind of scientist's slaying

The FBI was certain of Rita Gluzman's guilt, but could they prove it?
Rockland Journal News, April 20, 1996

Trial

Rita Gluzman went on trial at the courthouse in White Plains, NY on January 6, 1997, still maintaining her innocence and claiming she had no motive for killing Yakov. The first of 55 prosecution witnesses to take the stand was a private detective who had been hired by Rita to essentially stalk and harass Yakov and his girlfriend, Raisa Korenblitt. Then the jury would go on to hear about Rita's extravagance—such as her $3,200 refrigerator—and how nothing ever seemed enough for her. They would hear how she flew into a rage when Yakov left her and asked for a divorce. They would also hear testimony about Rita trying to ruin Raisa by planting cocaine on her, and sending extortion letters to Yakov's family. To the jury, this all must have seemed like an abundance of motive, but they would need something concrete about her actions involving the actual murder, too.

A witness at the Celia Gardens apartments stated that around 3am the night of the murder, she had looked out her window and saw a man and a woman loading plastic bags into the trunks of two cars. An employee of the CVS pharmacy identified Rita Gluzman as the woman who bought $32.02 worth of bandages and other medical supplies at 4am—supplies that were later found in Zelenin's car, and surveillance cameras had also captured her on video in the store. Then came the testimony for which everyone had been waiting, that of Vladimir Zelenin himself.

Zelenin was not only Rita's cousin, he was her employee at ECI, which in addition to his salary, provided him with a car and an apartment. He had two sons that depended on him, and he desperately didn't want them to go back to the Soviet Union, so when Rita came to him and said they would lose everything if he didn't help her kill Yakov, he felt it was his only course of action.

According to a *New York Times* article, Zelenin also described how he and Rita "calmly shopped for murder weapons at Home Depot, picking out an ax and a hacksaw," and "We discussed that we were going to do it together and for this we will need some other instruments, and we decided to take a hammer and a knife." They also "stopped at Grand Union for garbage bags," to dispose of Yakov's body.

Throughout her cousin's testimony—and indeed, throughout the trial—Rita displayed a variety of theatrics which included sobbing, appearing to faint, and shouting obscenities at the witnesses, but despite all of these distractions the truth continued to pour out like concrete walls of a prison cell forming around her.

Zelenin's most chilling testimony came as he described how they stood in the darkness of Celia Gardens apartment 223G, waiting for their prey, and struck him down the moment Yakov entered. Zelenin went into detail about his last "gurgling breath," and how after Yakov was dead, he began dismembering him: he first cut off Yakov's left leg below the knee, then the right leg, then the arm at the shoulder, and then Yakov's head.

It appeared as if the prosecution testimony of Zelenin and the other witnesses butchered any chance the defense team had of getting an acquittal, but still they hammered away at the star witness, trying to paint him as a liar. They brought up the fact that he had made up stories about his wife's death in the Soviet Union and threats against him and his sons in order to get into this country.

"You stood face to face with a professional interviewer and told that person lies, falsehoods, inaccuracies and misrepresentations?" defense attorney Hocheiser asked Zelenin.

"I had no other choice," Zelenin replied.

Perhaps this was the only strategy the defense had in the face of the evidence, but trying to assert that Zelenin's account of Rita's part in the murder plot could not be trusted, because he had lied to immigration officials to get his sons away from the oppression of the Soviet Union and bring them to freedom in the United States, didn't hold much water. Had Zelenin committed an unspeakable crime? Without question. Had Zelenin fabricated every word about Rita's motives and actions in the gruesome murder of her husband? Unlikely.

On January 28, the defense team began two long days of closing arguments. They again argued that their client had no reason to kill Yakov, and that he was worth more to her alive than dead. Zelenin was a proven liar, and he had committed the murder with an unknown accomplice.

Had the defense planted enough seeds of reasonable doubt? Juries often made inconceivable decisions, so the atmosphere in the courtroom was tense when the verdict was about to be read on January 30, 1997, after nearly ten hours of deliberation.

Silence filled the courtroom after Rita Gluzman was found guilty on all counts for the murder of her husband, Yakov Gluzman. That silence was only broken as the 40-year-old Zelenin looked at the woman who had essentially ended his life, too, and said in a loud voice, "Fuck you, bitch!"

Friday, January 31, 1997   THE PHILADELPHIA INQUIRER   ● City — **B3**

Wife found guilty in slaying, dismemberment of husband

Her cousin, a confessed accomplice, said she feared a coming divorce would curtail her spending habits.

for air before dying. Zelenin testified that while Rita Gluzman wiped up her husband's blood, he used ...

nounced in Russian, "When you kill, you cannot cry."
Zelenin, who testified through a ...

aminer said the autopsy was the greatest challenge of her career; after trying to reconstruct the body.

Because Rita Gluzman had crossed state lines, going from her home in Upper Saddle River in Ber...

Sentencing and Punishment

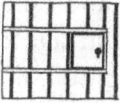

"For 25 years she gradually demolished him emotionally and in the 26th year she dismembered him physically," Yakov's parents wrote in a letter that was read at Rita's sentencing on April 30, 1997. The letter continued by addressing the damage to their grandson, as well. "By her evil act Rita has ruined the life of her son, whom she left fatherless, and marked him with the stigma of a mother convicted for murder."

U.S. District Court Judge Barrington D. Parker also weighed in with the following statement:

"None of us can ever know what transpired between you and your husband. The only thing we can know with any certainty is that nothing that occurred can possibly justify what you did to him. You are a woman of considerable courage, capacity and accomplishment. For whatever reasons, you allowed yourself to disintegrate around the relationship and the pain that grew out of that relationship."

Rita Gluzman, with tears in her eyes, simply stated, "I did not do that, and I still say that in front of the world."

The judge saw no reason for leniency in this brutal murder case, and he sentenced her to life in prison without the possibility of parole. In 1999, the U.S. Supreme Court refused to hear Rita Gluzman's appeal. She is currently in the FMC (Federal Medical Center) Carswell, in Fort Worth, Texas.

As for ECI, the company Rita was sure would fail without Yakov's money and help, it is still in business and being run by Rita's sister. Her son, Ilan, has also been working there for over 20 years.

Vladimir Zelenin was given a lighter sentence of 22½ years for cooperating with authorities. He was actually granted parole and released from prison in 2016.

Defense Attorney Michael Rosen, who passed away in 2017, continued to be bothered by the federal charges brought against Rita, which he described as hitting him "like a bullet."

"I've debated this in law schools ever since," he said years after the trial. "If this case didn't have that Violence Against Women Act, it would never have been tried. There was no physical evidence tying her to this crime. There wasn't one bit of forensics. The only evidence against Rita was her cousin's testimony and because he was an accomplice, his testimony alone would not enable state prosecutors in Rockland County to even indict her."

Rosen's attitude remains one of the more disturbing aspects of this extremely disturbing case, as it exemplifies how the law often has absolutely nothing to do with justice. Perhaps Rita didn't leave a fingerprint on the ax handle, but consider all of these points, which apparently were inconsequential to Rosen:

- Rita, consumed with jealousy and hatred, had more than enough motive and had already hired someone to harass Yakov and his girlfriend
- A witness at Celia Gardens saw a man *and a woman* loading garbage bags into the trunks of cars the night of the murder.
- Rita was identified at the CVS and *caught on camera* buying medical supplies right after the murder, supplies which were used to bandage Zelenin's wounded hand.
- Rita ran away after the murder and disappeared for 6 days. When she was found in Long Island she had travel brochures and stolen license plates, and had dyed her hair to change her appearance—actions not in keeping with an innocent woman, or a grief-stricken widow.
- Her own cousin, Vladimir Zelenin, gave a detailed account of Rita's thoughts, motives, and actions in the planning and literal execution of the heinous crime—none of which contradicted any of the known facts of the case, and in fact, explained everything.

Unfortunately, there will probably always be people who commit awful acts of violence, and we can only hope that law enforcement and the court system will act to the best of their ability to apprehend, prosecute, and punish the offenders. The families and friends of the victims deserve nothing less. The victims, such as Dr. Yakov Gluzman, deserve justice. It is up to the reader to decide if justice was served in this case.

Getting Away with Murder

Crime Scene

When Columbia County Undersheriff James Bertram crawled under the porch of the log home on Maple Drive in East Chatham, NY sometime after 11pm on the night of December 13, 1986, he was responding to a call from Vivian Gates. Vivian lived in a large white house next door to her son Robert, and she reported a shooting and possible multiple deaths at his house.

Peering through a window, Bertram saw the body of a woman at the base of the staircase. Making his way to another window, he saw the body of a man. As bad as the sight of these two victims was, however, what he saw next was even more disturbing—the body of a very small boy who was lying in front of a television which was still on. The toddler must have been innocently watching that television without a care in the world when the assailant killed him. What kind of monster could do such a thing to a child?

The Gates' log home.
Photos courtesy of the Columbia County Sheriff's Office

Once deputies arrived on the scene, the members of the sheriff's department entered the house and saw the horrors up close. There on the floor were the bloodied bodies of the woman, the man, who had a telephone nearby as if he had tried to call for help, and the heartbreaking scene of the toddler, who couldn't have been much more than three years old. But that was not all. In a rec room above the garage, they discovered yet another body; a young man lying next to a set of drums. The wounds all appeared to be gunshot wounds, and the shell casings found in the rec room and in the main house seemed to confirm that hypothesis.

The dining room where the Gates family ate their last meal
just before the murders occurred.

More law enforcement personnel continued to arrive at the Maple Drive house, as did both the District Attorney Eugene Keeler and the Assistant District Attorney. Keeler said of the scene, "It was very tragic, very sad, cold and calculating, whatever was done. Seeing the 3½ year old in front of the TV set with snow on it, that bothered me."

For others who were involved in the crime scene, they would say it was unlike anything they had ever witnessed. Sheriff Proper said it was worse than anything he had seen in Korea. Someone had methodically shot and killed 39-year-old Robert Gates, Sr., his 36-year-old girlfriend, Cheryl Brahm, 19-year-old Robert, Jr., and Robert Sr.'s 3-year-old grandson, Jason. An entire family had been murdered…well, not exactly the entire family.

Robert's other son, Wyley, a 17-year-old, Chatham High School student, was an intelligent "computer whiz" who resented having to work in his father's decidedly blue collar trucking business. Wyley generally acted cold and distant, and some suspected he had serious psychological issues. Soon, they would suspect him of much more than that.

Wyley Gates was the one who discovered the bodies, and then went next door to his grandmother's house to tell her that everyone had been shot and killed. Where had Wyley been when the crimes were being committed, and could a 17-year-old be capable of assassinating his own family?

Investigation

At 11pm, Walter Shook received a call to inform him of the multiple murders at the Gates home. Shook was a criminal investigator with the Columbia County Sheriff's Office, and he would be the first person to question Vivian Gates and her grandson, Wyley.

Shook found the two sitting on a couch at Vivian's house, where they had been waiting after she called the sheriff's department to report the awful crime. Wyley said he had discovered the bodies, and Shook then asked him to describe the events of the night. With no emotion, the boy calmly related that after his family finished their dinner of spaghetti and meatballs, he borrowed Cheryl Brahm's car and picked up his friend, Damian Rossney. They went to the Crandall Theater in Chatham to see Clint Eastwood's new movie, *Heartbreak Ridge*.

Wyley then went on to state that after the movie, he went to the house of Sally and Stanley Joseph, Damian's aunt and uncle, with whom he lived, to play some video games. Wyley claimed he tried calling home, but got a busy signal. He left the Joseph house about 10:30pm, and arrived home roughly 15 minutes later. The first body he found was that of his brother, Robert, Jr., in the rec room. Feeling for a pulse, he realized his brother was dead.

Apparently not concerned that the assailant might still be in the house, Wyley said he continued to go through the house and came upon his father, Robert, Sr., Cheryl, and his small nephew, Jason, also finding them to be dead. He then drove next door to his grandmother's house. As he stood in Vivian Gates' garage at 10:45pm, patting her German shepherd, she opened the door to see who was there. At this point, Wyley told her, "They're all dead." Shocked, and thinking there must have been a terrible accident to claim all four lives, Wyley corrected his grandmother and said there hadn't been any accident, that they had all been shot.

For some reason, Vivian did not call the sheriff's department until 10:56pm. When she tried to tell the officer that four people had been shot, he initially thought it was a crank call. After all, things like that just didn't happen in this town. Then Wyley got on the phone and confirmed what his grandmother had been saying, and was "coherent" enough to point out that he had been at the movies at the time of the shooting, he didn't see a gun in the house, and there were no other cars beside the truck his father owned.

Considering his family had just been murdered, and he had discovered the bloody scene, Wyley's "calm" recitation of the events raised a lot of red flags for Shook. What also drew suspicion was a bandage on Wyley's right thumb, but he explained to Shook he had simply closed his thumb in Cheryl's car door.

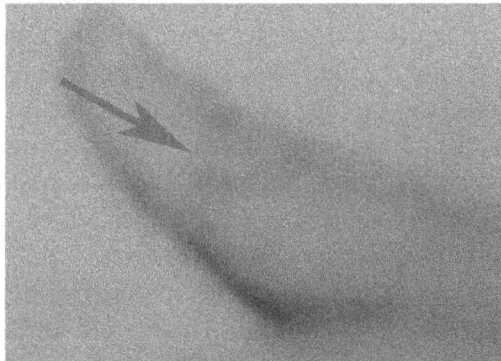

Despite the poor quality of the photo, the cut on Wyley's thumb is visible.

While Wyley quickly emerged as a prime suspect, investigators also knew that a burglary had occurred at the Gates house on December 4, just nine days earlier, and that guns had been among the items stolen. Had the burglars returned, and used the stolen weapons to kill everyone?

While this information could have started the investigation down the path of the "unknown assailant," that path actually circled right back to Wyley Gates:

- During the daytime burglary, the only room left untouched was Wyley's room.
- Wyley Gates was absent from school on December 4 when the burglary occurred.
- Among the items stolen were several weapons, one of which was a Walther PPK .380, which was known for "slide bite," which causes a cut on the thumb when fired, just like the wound Wyley claimed had been caused by the car door.

While the investigation and questions went on at the two Maple Drive homes, John Cozzolino of the Columbia County Sheriff's Office went to the Joseph residence about 12:30am to question Wyley's 16-year-old friend, Damian. For the most part, the boy gave the same story as to the sequence of events from the time Wyley picked him up for the movie, to the time he left after playing video games. There were a few slight discrepancies, however, such as whether or not Wyley had gotten a Band Aid for his thumb at the Joseph house, and the nature of the phone call Wyley had placed to Damian before arriving. Damian adamantly stated that he had absolutely no knowledge of the murders.

Damian's story changed, however, when police found the murder weapon, the Walther PPK, in his bedroom. Then he claimed that Wyley gave him the gun and told him about the murders, but he didn't really believe that Wyley had actually done it.

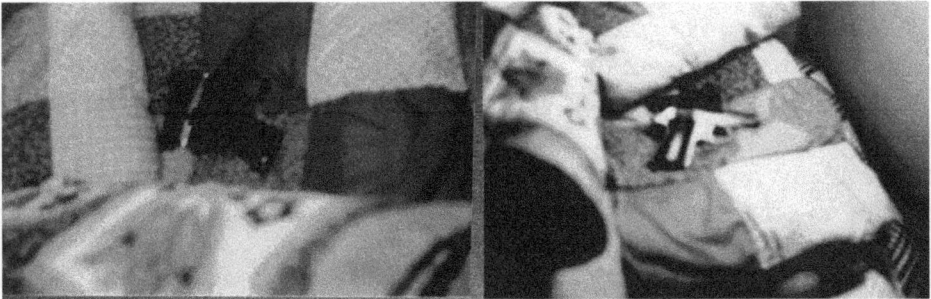

Guns found in Damian's room, including
the murder weapon, the Walther PPK.

Back at Vivian's house, stunned friends and family began gathering. In the midst of all the shock and grief, Shook asked Wyley to write down everything he had said about the night's events, which he did in great detail, considering the circumstances. Wyley was even able to describe the locations and positions of all of the bodies.

After completing his statement, Wyley was questioned further, and he agreed to go take a polygraph. Shook and Cozzolino both accompanied him to the Chatham police station, where lawyer Richard Hogle, who had previously done some work for the Gates family regarding custody of little Jason, would arrive to ensure Wyley's rights were being protected. Then Shook drove Wyley and his lawyer to Poughkeepsie, to the Troop K Barracks of the New York State Police, where Thomas Salmon of the Bureau of Criminal Investigation would administer the polygraph examination.

After signing a permission form, which was witnessed by Hogle, Wyley began the pre-test part of the polygraph, which was observed by Shook and Trooper Bernard Keller. Salmon asked a series of general pre-test questions, but before he could get to the serious questions about the crime during the actual test, Wyley made a stunning statement.

"I planned it and I killed them," Wyley stated, according to Salmon and the other two witnesses.

Wyley went on to confess that he had practiced firing the Walter PPK, which he had stolen from his own house. He had originally only intended to kill his "worthless" brother and his father, who he claimed caused him so much stress. Instead, he shot his father three times as the wounded man tried reaching for the phone. He also shot Cheryl three times, and when she tried to crawl up the staircase, he shot her again. Later, he shot both his father and Cheryl one more time each.

Going to the rec room, where his brother was playing the drums, he entered and at a distance of just 6 feet, began shooting. Wyley added that as he was firing, his brother yelled, "You stupid fool!" That was something his brother had often said to him, and it always made him very angry. Now it would be his brother's last words.

Finally, Wyley described young Jason, who was in front of the television, screaming and crying from all of the gunshots. He couldn't recall at what point he actually shot the little boy, but he did describe why he murdered the child—to keep him from being a witness, and also to prevent him from sharing in the inheritance Wyley expected to get.

There were the motives; Wyley wanted to eliminate the family he hated and inherit what he thought was a large estate.

Wyley also said that his friend, Damian, had been in on the burglary to steal the guns, and knew all about the murder plot.

Salmon then asked, point for point, if Wyley had planned and committed these murders, and he replied, "Yes" to every question. However, when Salmon asked if he could then begin the actual polygraph test so Wyley could repeat the admissions he had freely made, Wyley surprised them yet again.

"If I do, it would be bad for me. If I don't, I might have a chance."

So the official polygraph exam never commenced and Wyley's confession had not been taped or written down. But still, he had openly— and in great detail— admitted to murdering his family in front of two New York State Police officers, and a sheriff's department investigator. And, Wyley had the exact wound on his thumb

Wiley Gates, 17, is escorted from the Columbia County Sheriff's Office Sunday after being charged with the murder of four family members. (AP Laserphoto)

17-year-old charged with killing family

Post-Star headline December 15, 1986

21

which would be caused by firing the Walter PPK. He had motive and he had opportunity. Surely, this would be enough to convict this cold, calculating monster who had slaughtered his family in cold blood out of greed and hatred.

At 10:30am on December 14, Wyley was arrested. All that seemed left was the formality of a trial before sending this assassin to prison for the rest of his life.

Trial

"Back in October and November of 1986, Mr. Gates started thinking of hatred, murder and money."

And so began the trial of Wyley Gates on Monday, August 17, 1987, with the opening statement of DA Keeler. Defense Attorney Charles Wilcox countered by declaring that the members of the jury would "have many and deep reasonable doubts about who shot Robert Gates, Sr., Robert, Jr., Jason Gates, and Cheryl Brahm" by the time the trial drew to a close. The blame, and guilt, according to Wilcox, for these crimes rested squarely on the shoulders of Wyley's supposed friends, Damian Rossney, and Miles McDonald. Both boys had been part of the burglary to steal the guns, and one of *them* may have actually pulled the trigger, according to Wilcox.

If that strategy didn't work, Wilcox also laid the groundwork for an insanity defense in his opening statement. He would throw everything out there for this case and hope that something would stick.

With every witness called by the prosecution, in Wilcox's cross examination he seemingly grasped at straws, nitpicking at minutiae, but all the while cleverly amassing little bits of possible doubt. While on the one hand, he appeared to base the defense on the bad influence of Damian and Miles, and Wyley's insanity, which made him not responsible for any act of violence he may have committed, Wilcox would also emphasize that Wyley was incapable of doing any act of violence. It seemed impossible that playing both sides of the fence had any chance of succeeding with the jury, especially given Wyley's confession, but Wilcox continued day after day and week after week to methodically hammer away.

As for that alleged confession by his client, Wilcox asserted that it could all have been concocted by the various law enforcement personnel and fed to the impressionable and vulnerable Wyley. Wilcox also claimed there were discrepancies in the forensic evidence that didn't mesh with Wyley's account of the murders. He further drove home the point that law enforcement failed to properly collect and test potential evidence that might have exonerated his client, and that overall they had done an inadequate job investigating this case.

If the jury was to believe Wilcox, as the long, hot days dragged on into autumn, the prosecution had no evidence proving that a mentally unbalanced Wyley Gates pulled the trigger, and Wyley's confession was a total fabrication. But would anyone buy such obvious legal maneuverings and nonsense?

A very long nine weeks and 49 witnesses later, and the prosecution and defense finally made their closing remarks on October 1. Judge Leaman then gave two hours of detailed instructions to the jury, and they would finally begin their deliberations at 5pm.

In what was later described by jury members as a tense atmosphere, or a downright "battle," they argued and shouted back and forth as to whether or not the prosecution had met its burden of proof. On the night of October 6, the jury finally had a unanimous decision, and at 10:30pm the courtroom began to fill to hear the verdict.

As the judge asked about each count of the murder indictments, the foreman replied "Not guilty." It seemed impossible, inconceivable, but the defense team had managed to wriggle their way through the slime of what all too often passes for justice in this country. The only count which returned a verdict of guilty was second-degree conspiracy to commit murder. Everyone in the courtroom was shocked and silent. They say justice is blind, but in the Wyley Gates' case it also appeared to be deaf and dumb.

Sentencing and Punishment

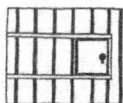

As everyone awaited the sentencing on November 9, punishments were already being handed out—to the members of the jury. Harassing phone calls to their homes began immediately, some even threatening death, and they went on month after month. While some people in town blamed an inadequate police investigation and the understaffed District Attorney's office for this travesty of justice, many blamed the jury for missing the obvious facts and being swayed by Wilcox's legal sleight of hand to misdirect them. Cheryl Brahm's brother, Peter, summed up what just about everyone was feeling.

"I don't think there's a person in Columbia County who thinks he didn't do it, except those twelve people."

Even Wyley Gates' grandmother, Vivian, had fully expected guilty, but insane, verdicts on the murder charges. Remarkably, despite her grandson murdering her family members, she reacted to the not guilty verdicts by commenting, "But now that it's over and I've thought about it, for Wyley it's good. He'll have a better opportunity to accomplish something than in a mental institution."

What about the opportunities her own son, Robert. Sr., would never have, or her grandson, Robert, Jr.? And was she even able to overlook the opportunity to simply grow up that Wyley took from her 3-year-old grandson, Jason?

SUNDAY DEMOCRAT AND CHRONICLE, ROCHESTER, N.Y., OCTOBER 18, 1987 **NEW YORK 27A**

Acquittal in 'crime of the century' leaves Columbia County in chaos

Jurors disregarded confession in trial of Wyley Gates, 17

By Sara Rimer
The New York Times

CANAAN — Less than a week after four people were shot to death in their home here last winter, the case that Columbia County investigators were calling the

partment, even as the trial has posed serious questions about the investigation. And everyone is left wondering whether anyone will ever be convicted of the murders.

The members of the jury called their verdict the most agonizing decision of their lives, one with painful repercussions in a community where it is hard to remain anonymous.

What it came down to, according to jurors who were inter-

sions in the school cafeteria and the computer room.

The details of the plan kept changing, testified McDonald, who was granted immunity in exchange for his testimony.

On Dec. 4, nine days before the murders, the three classmates staged a burglary at the Gates house. McDonald testified that Rossney broke into the gun cabinet, taking what eventually became the murder weapon, a Wal-

movie. The police recovered the gun at Rossney's house.

Rossney, who is free on bail and attending high school, is scheduled for trial this winter on charges of second-degree murder and conspiracy to commit murder.

Gates' lawyer, Charles Wilcox, presented as witnesses two psychiatrists and one psychologist who testified that Gates was psychotic. He argued that Gates was a fragile young man who was capable of be-

ey or for the thrill of killing.

From the beginning, the police based their case on Gates' confession. During the trial, however, it came out that the confession consisted of rough notes and the investigators' recollection of what Gates had said under questioning.

Furthermore, earlier on the night of the murders, Gates had given a written statement that he was not the killer.

There were apparent lapses in

subjected to laboratory tests for gunpowder residue. The police said they chose to test the blood on the gun rather than fingerprinting it. Both tests, they said, could not be done. The blood test showed only that the blood was human but did not specify type.

Wilcox argued in court that the case was built on overzealous and misguided police work based too much on investigators' impressions of Wyley Gates as a strange youth

Headlines from the *Democrat and Chronicle* and *Daily News*.

Jury clears whiz kid of 4 murders

By LARRY COLE
and JOSEPH McNAMARA
Daily News Staff Writers

The Columbia County jury that acquitted Wyley Gates of murder in the massacre of his family had trouble accepting his confession to the grisly crime, his attorney declared yesterday.

After 63 hours of deliberation over six days, the jury found Gates, 18-year-old former high school honor student, innocent of four murder counts Tuesday night in Hudson, 20 miles from Albany.

The six men and six women convicted him of conspiracy to murder, which carries a maximum sentence of 8⅓ to 25 years. He will be sentenced Nov. 9.

Defense attorney Charles Wilcox called the acquittal a "victory for the Constitution," and evidence that Gates' rights had been trammeled.

Gates confessed to the pistol slayings of his father, Robert Sr., 39; brother, Robert Jr., 19; cousin Jason, 3, and the elder Gates' live-in girl friend, Cheryl Braham, 36, in the family's log-house home last Dec. 13. The massacre rocked rural East Chatham, 14 miles from Hudson.

But his admission was made to a private polygraph operator, not a policeman, and was made without an attorney present, Wilcox declared.

"It (the verdict) sends a message to police that ... when you don't abide by the Constitution and make a legitimate arrest, it won't stick," Wilcox said.

The jury obviously gagged on this issue. In the final day of pondering, the panel asked County Judge John Leaman to explain the factors needed for a voluntary confession. Later the same day it asked for a repeat of Leaman's 20-minute explanation.

Wilcox claimed at trial that Gates was not the actual shooter (another defendant, Damian Rossney, 17, formerly of East Chatham, now of Ossining, will stand trial on the same charges this winter), and that Gates was legally insane.

"He's never expressed emotion about the four deaths," Wilcox told the Daily News yesterday.

"If Wyley is sentenced to prison, as I expect he will be, we're going to recommend that he be given psychiatric treatment and counseling," said Wilcox.

Wyley Gates

The lives of the jurors were changed forever, as were the lives of so many people in Columbia County, and not for the better. On the morning of sentencing on November 9, the question remained—was there *any* justice to be had for the four innocent victims of this brutal crime?

From the start, Judge Leaman made it clear that leniency would not be the order of the day when he stated, "The motivation for the conspiracy stemmed directly from the defendant's dissatisfaction, even to the point of hatred, for a member of his family, namely his father. His hatred gave birth to this conspiracy, which was achieved in the end, and I conclude that to a moral certainty." He then sentenced Wyley to a state prison term of no less than eight and one third to twenty-five years, and Wyley was soon taken to Elmira Correctional Facility to begin serving his sentence.

On November 22, 1988, Wyley's friend and partner in crime, Damian Rossney, also went on trial for murder and conspiracy. Would someone finally pay for these crimes? On December 7, once again, a jury arrived at verdicts of not guilty on the murder charges, but guilty for conspiracy to commit murder and criminal facilitation. On February 7, 1989, Rossney was sentenced to eight and one third to twenty-five years for conspiracy, and five to fifteen years for criminal facilitation, but to be served concurrently.

As if the huge financial strain of the murder investigation and trials had not been enough of a burden on the taxpayers of Columbia County, they were also to be stuck with the bill of paying for Wyley Gates' college education while he was in prison. After serving just seventeen years of his sentence, a parole board actually released him for "good behavior" on August 12, 2003. Using his free college degree and years of firsthand legal experience, Wyley landed a job with a law firm in New York City.

Damian Rossney is also now a free man.

Amidst all the understandable outrage involving this case, when asked about it years later, Wilcox reiterated how proud he was that the jury upheld Wyley Gates' constitutional rights!

Perhaps Chief Shatney of the East Chatham Fire Department—where Robert, Jr. was a member—said it best.

"I don't think there is any justice in Columbia County."

Unfortunately, that problem is not limited to just this case or Columbia County.

The Perfect Crime...Almost

Crime Scene

To the casual observer in 1903, there was no crime scene.

While the exterior of the old house in Centreville, NY, (now Woodridge) was run down and shabby, the interior had received a fresh coat of paint and some new wallpaper—but that was only to conceal the bloodstains on the floor and the bullet holes in the walls.

If you knew exactly where to look, all that remained of Lafayette "Lafe" Taylor's body were some burnt bones buried under a pile of manure. The smaller bones had been ground up and mixed with the ashes of his flesh and had been fed to the chickens.

Investigation

Initially, there were no suspects as no one knew a crime had been committed. Even Lafe's friends agreed he was a "shiftless backwoodsman" who was "addicted to drink," and it would not have been out of character for him to take off for extended periods of time.

When did not show up for a job in early February, his wife, Kate, said he had gone to Orange County looking for work and had never returned. As there had been considerable turmoil and abuse in the marriage, it wasn't surprising to anyone that Lafe could have run out on his wife and 14-year-old stepdaughter, Ida May DeKay.

It was potentially a perfect crime, until Kate made an unusual declaration. She tried to sell Lafe's horse to a man in town, but the man was afraid that Lafe would return and demand his horse be given back to him. As Lafe was well known to be prone to violence, especially when drunk, the man did not want to risk buying the horse, even at a bargain price. Insistent that he purchase the animal, Kate said the oddest thing to "reassure" him. She told the man not to worry about Lafe returning, because she had killed him, and then cut up his body into little pieces and burned them!

It seemed impossible to believe, but the man went to the authorities just in the case there was a one in a million chance Kate was telling the truth about murdering her husband. Kate's daughter, Ida, was brought in for questioning, and at first was reluctant to speak against her mother. That reluctance quickly vanished, however, when she was offered the sum of five dollars to testify against her mother!

YOUNG GIRL TELLS OF MOTHER'S CRIME.

There should have been little need of any further investigation after Ida confirmed that Kate had killed Lafayette, and she then helped her mother butcher and burn the body, yet the district attorney could not believe the girl's story. How could anyone believe that a wife and young girl could do such a hideous and barbaric thing!?

DISTRICT ATTORNEY DOUBTS IDA TAYLOR'S STORY.

It is understood that District Attorney Anderson and those interested with him in securing all the evidence in the Lafayette Taylor murder case do not believe that all the body of the murdered man was burned by Mrs. Taylor.

Another article in the local paper spoke to the general belief that Lafe had indeed been murdered, but it seems no one put any credence in the gruesome confession. As a result, some of Lafe's friends were taking extreme measures in the search for his body:

A Middletown clairvoyant has been employed by the friends of the late "Lafe" Taylor to locate his body, the friends doubting the story of his daughter who said her mother chopped up the body and burned it in the stove. The clairvoyant says she knows what disposition was made of the body, but will not tell until properly compensated for her time and services.

Authorities were taking a more conservative route, asserting that Kate must have simply disposed of her husband's body in a local lake. Although the lake had several feet of ice on it, there was one section where some ice had been cut and removed. The surface had refrozen there, but only to a depth of a few inches.

The district attorney ordered that section of ice cut away, and the bottom of the lake dredged, but they found nothing. Unable to locate Taylor's body anywhere, authorities were forced to reexamine Kate's original confession, and Ida's story. There is that old saying that when all other possibilities can be dismissed, the one remaining, however unlikely, has to be the truth—and that truth was truly horrific.

The large bones in Lafe's body, which were so difficult to burn, were indeed found by authorities at the bottom of the manure pile. The investigation came to an end.

MRS. LAFAYETTE TAYLOR MURDERED HER HUSBAND

AND BURNED HIS BODY IN A COOK STOVE.

WOMAN HAS CONFESSED AND IS IN JAIL.

Trial

During the trial of Kate Taylor, her daughter Ida gave a detailed and chilling account of the events of that night. While her mother had claimed that Lafe had come home drunk and had started to beat her, Ida claimed that the couple was quietly drinking tea at the dining table when she went to bed. The next thing she knew, she was awakened by the sound of gunshots.

Hurrying to the kitchen, Ida stated that she found her mother chopping off Lafe's head and arm with an ax. Far from running screaming from the house, the girl then helped cut up the body up with that ax, storing the pieces in a basin in the pantry. Over the course of several days, they would put a few more chunks into the wood stove to burn the flesh and bones. The ashes and some of the smaller bones were ground up and then mixed with the chicken feed, and subsequently devoured. The larger bones were scorched, but not easy to grind, so they were buried beneath a manure pile.

HOW MRS. TAYLOR KILLED AND BURNED HER HUSBAND.

FIRST SHOT HIM AND THEN CUT OFF HIS HEAD.

TESTIMONY WHICH IMPRESSED THE JURY.

Ida even claimed that the morning after the murder, having just burned her husband's head and arm in the stove, Kate Taylor calmly made pancakes for breakfast on that very same stove! She went on to explain to the shocked jurors that wallpaper was used to cover the bullet holes, and a fresh coat of paint hid all the bloodstains.

Kate claimed that her actions were in self-defense, but stories emerged that she had already tried to murder her husband once before. While Lafe had been sleeping in the barn, Kate boarded the door and set fire to the building! In her defense, friends of Kate testified that they had witnessed Lafe regularly beating and abusing his wife, often knocking her to the floor. As part of the prosecution, friends of Lafe stated that he had numerous scars where Kate had beaten *him* with an ax handle!

The plot thickened even more when another man entered the legal scene. Local farmer Peter Yerkin was arrested and accused of not only being Kate's lover, but her co-conspirator. Some claimed that Yerkin had even been the driving force behind the murder, hounding Kate until she finally did his dirty work for him.

Kate went on the record in saying that someone else had been involved in the murder, although she didn't specifically name Yerkin. A neighbor testified that Yerkin knew all of the details of the murder before anyone else, and that Yerkin had threatened to do him harm if he told anyone about his involvement in the crime. Yet, loyal friends swore that Yerkin was a quiet, simple farmer who had been falsely accused.

Newspaper accounts described Yerkin as an emotional and physical wreck behind bars, breaking under the strain of his imprisonment and all the interrogations. While the rumor mill had no doubt of his guilt, ultimately, no substantial evidence could be produced, and Yerkin was set free. A newspaper article some years later reported that Yerkin had gotten married, so apparently he was able to get his life back in order.

> **Peter Yerkins, who is in Monticello jail, awaiting the action of the grand jury, on a charge of being an accessory to the murder of Lafayette Taylor, is said to be breaking down under the strain and weeps much of the time. Mrs. Taylor's jail life apparently agrees with her.**

Was Yerkin guilty, or innocent? He likely at least had prior knowledge of the crime, and perhaps some involvement. Ida had apparently said that right after the murder, her mother opened the front door and swung a lantern back and forth, as if signaling someone that the deed had been done. Of course, suspicions are one thing, and proof in a court of law is entirely different, so Yerkin was released.

However, while Yerkin walked, the jury did not buy Lafe's wife's claim of self-defense. Mrs. Kate Taylor was found guilty of first degree murder.

Sentencing and Punishment

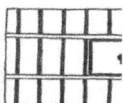

For her horrific crime, Kate was sentenced to death and sent to prison in Dannemora, New York, on June 2. Justice was to be swift, as she was scheduled to die in the electric chair the week of July 5, but within just a few days of being executed, she was granted a second trial.

This time she was only found guilty of second degree murder, and sent to the Matteawan State Hospital for the Criminally Insane in Fishkill,

New York. Although spared from execution, her health quickly deteriorated, and 44-year-old Kate Taylor died in prison in 1907.

Ida was never charged with any crime, even though she was clearly an accessory after the fact. Not too many 14-year-old girls would have had the intestinal fortitude to help cut up and burn their stepfather, and she never seems to have had any remorse for her actions, or sympathy for the victim. If Lafe was an abusive drunk, Ida was probably happy to see him go.

If Kate Taylor had kept her mouth shut, chances are no one would have even suspected this ghastly crime had been committed. And if authorities hadn't given Ida $5 to testify against her mother, who knows if the crime would have ever been solved!

Paroled Killer

Crime Scene

At about 9:30am on the morning of March 26, 1991, Lorraine Healy and Gregory Rooker were jogging along an abandoned railroad bed off Stanton Street in Middletown, NY, when they made a grisly discovery. There was the naked body of a white female who had been savagely stabbed. In addition to the over 30 stab wounds, her face had been slashed and her abdomen had been cut open. An autopsy later revealed that the victim was three months pregnant, and she had not been dead for more than a day or so. There was obviously a monster on the loose, but what was the identity of this victim?

Using "past police records and photographs," officials were able to identify the woman as 29-year-old Juliana Rose Frank of Middletown, an unemployed mother of two. Trying to piece together her whereabouts in the last days of her life, her stepfather and some friends mentioned seeing her in a couple of bars in town, and walking along North Street, but no solid leads developed. The case quickly went cold.

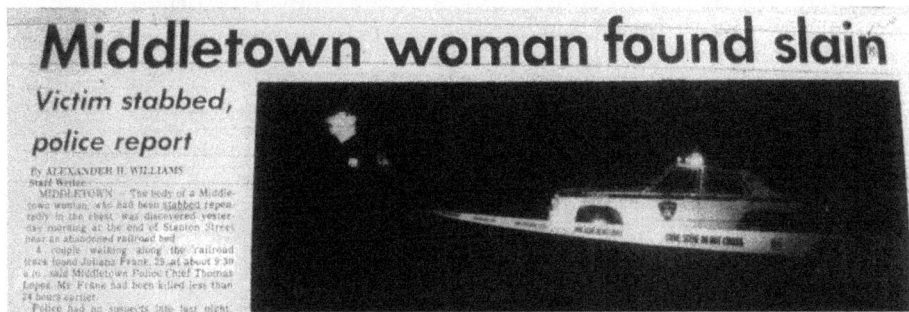

Middletown woman found slain

Victim stabbed, police report

By ALEXANDER H. WILLIAMS
Staff Writer
MIDDLETOWN — The body of a Middletown woman, who had been stabbed repeatedly in the chest, was discovered yesterday morning at the end of Stanton Street near an abandoned railroad bed.
A couple walking along the railroad tracks found Juliana Frank, 29, at about 9:30 a.m., said Middletown Police Chief Thomas Leppo. Ms. Frank had been killed less than 24 hours earlier.
Police had no suspects late last night.

Headline of the Frank murder in the *Times Herald Record*, March 27, 1991.

More than a year later, on July 1, 1992, 14-year-old Christine Klebbe of Carlos Drive in Goshen, NY was reported missing by her parents. Last seen on June 29, there was no sign of any foul play, and no one had seen anything suspicious—she simply disappeared. The family put up posters and spread the word that she was missing, but until there was some evidence of a crime, police had little to go on.

On July 10, 1992, Gary Young, a friend of 34-year-old Laurette Reviere Huggins, went to see her at 12:30pm at her apartment at 23 Bonnell Street in Middletown. Young was horrified to discover that Huggins had been viciously stabbed to death.

Two days later, the local *Times Herald Record* newspaper reported that:

Mrs. Huggins spoke with a slight Caribbean accent, was black with light skin, and stood 5 feet 6 inches tall, according to authorities and friends. She worked at the Blue Cross/Blue Shield office at Crystal Run.

Huggins had two daughters, ages 16 and 9, who were not home at the time of the murder, and also a son who was attending school on the island of St. Vincent, where Huggins originated, and where she was planning to return. In fact, she was in the process of packing to move back to her Caribbean home. Friends and neighbors described her as a very pleasant person who usually kept to herself. Of later significance, one friend noted that Huggins "walked a lot, and got rides from friends," but no solid suspects in the brutal crime emerged.

On July 20, cousins Angelina Hopkins, aged 23, of Poughkeepsie, NY, and Brenda Whiteside, 20, of Elmsford, NY, were having a good time at the club Bluenote at 117 N. Hamilton in Poughkeepsie. They were last seen leaving the bar with some men, and they never returned home. The following day, Angelina's mother, Anna Theresa, and her sister, Cecelia, filed missing persons reports.

On Thursday, July 30, a man was walking his dog near the burned and abandoned former Hillcrest Manor Restaurant off Harriman Drive in Goshen, when he found the naked body of a woman who had been stabbed to death. The body was identified as 27-year-old Adraine Hunter, a home health aide, who had been living with her grandmother and daughter on Sprague Street in Middletown.

Connections were finally beginning to be made, and the *Times Herald Record* noted in an article on August 2 that "the Hunter case is the third unsolved murder of Middletown women in a little more than a year's time. All three were single mothers stabbed to death." According to a *Journal News* article, the three women had also been raped. However, in a move that was later severely criticized, at no point had any warnings been posted by police of a possible serial killer operating in the area. In that same August 2 article, Middletown Mayor Gertrude Mokotoff defended the lack of any official announcement by saying, "I think there is something to be said for not alarming the public unduly."

So, while nothing was being said to "alarm" the public, the bodies of three women were found, and two other women and a teenager were missing. And it would not be the police who would break this case.

THE VICTIMS

CHRISTINE KIEBBE: *14, Goshen*

JULIANNA FRANK: *29, Middletown*

ANGELA HOPKINS: *23, Poughkeepsie*

ADRIANE HUNTER: *27, Middletown*

BRENDA WHITESIDE: *20, Elmsford*

LAURETTE HUGGINS REVIERE: *34, Middletown*

The six victims, *Rockland Journal News*, August 6, 1992

Investigation

"I couldn't sleep nights," Cecelia Hopkins said, after her sister and cousin disappeared.

Desperate for answers, and getting none from police, Cecelia and her mother decided to take matters into their own hands. As an August 6 *Times Herald Record* article stated:

Law enforcement and civic officials have long acknowledged an air of tension between the minority community and police.

Knowing that they would have a better chance of getting information from people in the local bars and on the street, Mrs. Hopkins, Cecelia, and other family members began questioning everyone who would speak to them. They discovered that Angelina and Brenda had left the Bluenote with four men, but they were only able to get the first names and nicknames of the men. They went to the police with this information, but were told that wasn't enough. So for the next two weeks, family members went to the club every night, hoping one or more of the men would show up again. Their efforts finally paid off.

Captain Donald Briggs of the Poughkeepsie Police Department stated, "We really didn't have much to do with breaking the case. It was mostly Mrs. Hopkins."

On August 2, Mrs. Hopkins called the police again and said that one of the men's names was White, and he was back at the Bluenote. Officer Robert Perrotta responded and found White in the club's parking lot.

"I'd like to speak to you," Perrotta said.

"I don't like speaking with cops," White responded.

According to the August 6 *Times Herald Record* article, the conversation continued:

"Well," Perrotta said, "this lady would like to talk with you," and indicated Mrs. Hopkins knew that White had been with her missing daughter and cousin.

White also told the officer he had been with the women, but had merely given them a ride to Middletown and had not seen them since.

According to Briggs, Perrotta left, and White later called Mrs. Hopkins. The extent of that conversation could not be learned yesterday.

When Perrotta got back to the Poughkeepsie police station, Briggs said, he noticed one missing teenager from the Middletown area, and that

36

another woman, Adraine Hunter, had been found dead days earlier in Goshen.

Because White was acting strangely, Perrotta called the state police, Briggs said.

Finally, the state police and local law enforcement had a prime suspect on their radar, Nathaniel White, a name that hadn't come up in any of the previous investigations. He was someone who had managed to evade suspicion, even from the woman he lived with, his girlfriend, Jill Garrison.

Garrison, who later claimed she "didn't see any clues" that her live-in boyfriend might be dangerous, said that she met White in 1986 and he "treated me like a lady." He gave her roses, and "helped clean the house, cook meals, and do the laundry." However, despite steadfastly maintaining that she didn't see "any signs," there were plenty of red flags over the course of the years.

In October of 1987, White was facing charges for an armed robbery (with a knife) of a convenience store in New Windsor, and for two other robberies in Middletown. He pleaded the charges down to a single count of second-degree robbery. Sentenced to 3 to 9 years, he was later granted a "certificate of eligibility" by the Department of Correctional Services, which led to his early release in 1989, at which point, Jill Garrison took him back into her home.

In 1990, White was next charged with assault and resisting arrest, which should have brought stiff penalties as he was on parole. However, the parole board was never informed of his arrest, and he avoided jail by pleading guilty to misdemeanor disorderly conduct. After paying a fine of only $142, White was released.

Jill Garrison introduced her friend, Juliana R. Frank, to White, and Frank was murdered in March of 1991.

In April of 1991, White was charged with the kidnapping and assault—at knifepoint—of a 16-year-old girl.

"I'm sure he would have killed me. I'm sure," the girl, who asked to remain anonymous, later said.

The young girl was at the Moonbeams dance club on Route 211 in Middletown when Nathaniel White offered her a ride home. White used to "fool around" with one of her friends, so he was no stranger, and she accepted his offer. However, instead of taking her home, he pulled into a parking lot on Mount Hope Road and pulled out a knife.

"He grabbed the back of my head and pushed it into his lap," the girl said, "and he told me 'Don't talk, don't do nothing. I'll cut you. I'm going to take you back to my house and you're gonna do whatever I want you to do.' "

Still threatening to cut her, White then drove to his apartment in a house on Reinhardt Road in the Town of Wallkill. Bringing her to the front porch of the house, White told her to stay there while he checked to make sure no one was inside.

"When I come back out if you're not here I'm going to kill you," White said.

Fortunately, the girl had the presence of mind to run for her life, literarily, and she raced across a field to the home of Regina Fiumarelli, screaming for help. At first fearful that this might be some home invasion ploy, Fiumarelli nonetheless opened her door to the hysterical girl and called the police.

For this latest crime, White could have been sentenced to 25 years. As an ex-convict out on parole, he would have had to serve a minimum of 12 years for charges which could have included kidnapping, assault, and attempted rape. Instead, an overburdened court system let White plea down to a charge of unlawful imprisonment and he served only nine months. It is inconceivable—threatening to rape and murder a 16-year-old girl and getting just nine months! It was "like a slap on the wrist" the girl's mother said.

After White's release on April 23, 1992 with his second parole, Jill Garrison once again let White move back in. When asked why she took him back after such a heinous crime, especially as she had children of her own, Garrison responded that "he didn't do anything to me. I loved him then." However, conversely, she also admitted that when White got angry "he hit me, but not to the extent that you would see it."

Just two months after his release, the savage killing spree would begin, and the next victim would be Garrison's own niece, 14-year-old Christine Klebbe. Just days after she disappeared, White and Garrison went to the Klebbe's 4th of July party, where White assured Christine's father, Christopher (who was also Jill's brother), that Christine was okay and would turn up soon. White even claimed that a friend told him that he recently saw Christine at the Galleria Mall in Middletown.

Christopher would later tell reporters that White "always talked about women. He talked about the things he wanted to do to them—sexual things. He was constantly obsessed by it."

A week later, Laurette Huggins—one of Garrison's closest friends, whom she had also introduced to White—was murdered in her own house. Garrison would later tell reporters that when they heard the news, she and White expressed concern over what would happen to Huggins' two daughters, who had just spent the night at their house a few weeks earlier.

Ten days later, cousins Angelina Hopkins, who was also a mother, of a 7-month-old child, and Brenda Whiteside, accepted a ride from Nathaniel White at the Bluenote in Poughkeepsie. White had graduated from high school in Poughkeepsie in 1979. The two women were never seen alive again.

Just ten days after that, Adraine Hunter was found murdered. That same day, White was fired from his job at a factory for coming in late.

If not for Mrs. Hopkins and her daughter, Cecelia, the slaughter would no doubt have continued at a terrifying pace, as White's parole officer, the police, the prison system, and his own girlfriend had no clue as to what a monster White had become. When later criticized for the complete failure of the criminal justice system to keep this violent offender behind bars and properly assess his mental state, Orange County District Attorney Francis Phillips pointed out that his office handled thousands of cases a year and he told reporters, "I'm not God."

On August 3, 1992, the New York State Police brought in 32-year-old Nathaniel White for questioning. While all the signs pointed to White's guilt, there was a lack of forensic evidence to prove he actually committed any of the murders. It would have been a very difficult case to prosecute, and there was a good chance that a clever lawyer would have been able to set his client free.

Then White did something that other serial killers have been known to do—he confessed to all six murders, perhaps as a twisted way to boast about his bloody accomplishments. On August 4, he even led police to the site on Echo Lake Drive in Goshen where he had dumped Christine Klebbe's body, and to the abandoned house on Harriman Drive in Goshen where he left the bodies of Angelina Hopkins and Brenda Whiteside outside, near a shed. He also led them to some of the victims' clothing, and the weapons he used to stab, bludgeon, and mutilate the women. And because bragging to the police wasn't good enough, he granted an interview to WNBC-TV, which was also attended by a reporter from the *Times Herald Record*.

White claimed that voices told him to hurt women, and he got his ideas for killing from violent movies like *Robocop*.

"The first girl I killed [Juliana Frank] was from a *Robocop* movie...I seen him cut somebody's throat, then take the knife and slit down the chest to the stomach and then left the body in a certain position. With the first person I killed, I did exactly what I saw in the movie...Once I got so much alcohol in me, I just snapped. I couldn't control it...I would ... see something violent happen, and it seems to just sink in."

ORANGE COUNTY KILLINGS

'Once they got in the car . . . I fought with myself.
Part of me didn't want to do it, part of me did, O.K.?'
— Nathaniel White in interview

Accused killer: I just snapped

Carole Tanzer Miller
d John Reinan
ff Writers

MIDDLETOWN — Accused ial killer Nathaniel White yesday said voices in his head de him slay five women and a n-age girl and leave their bodscattered around southern nge County.

Police said White, 32, a crimiparolee, has confessed to all killings, including that of 20-ir-old Brenda Whiteside of nsford. Yesterday, White told Yew York City television sta1 that he was responding to lers from inner voices that he ght, but ultimately obeyed.

"I didn't want to do it. Each ie I did it, it was like I wasn't self, I was someone else. . . . I

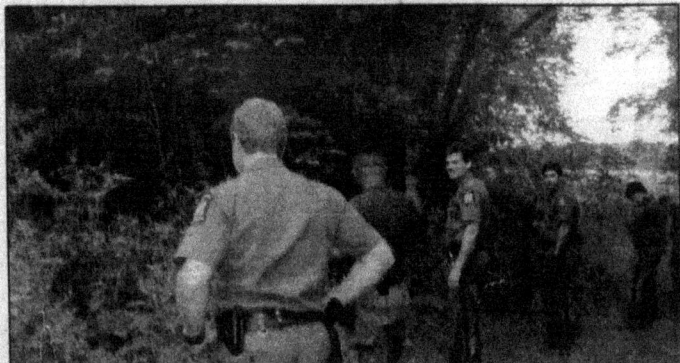

Rockland Journal News, August 6, 1992

40

White explained that he would be drinking and a voice would tell him to "go out for a drive." Once he had found a woman, usually at a bar, he would offer her a ride. He then stated that one voice would be telling him to leave her alone, while another voice would be saying, "She doesn't deserve to live. You should hit her."

Regardless of whether or not these alleged voices were just setting the stage for an insanity plea, he went on to repeat his confession to all six murders. He even stated how much he "enjoyed" the actual killings.

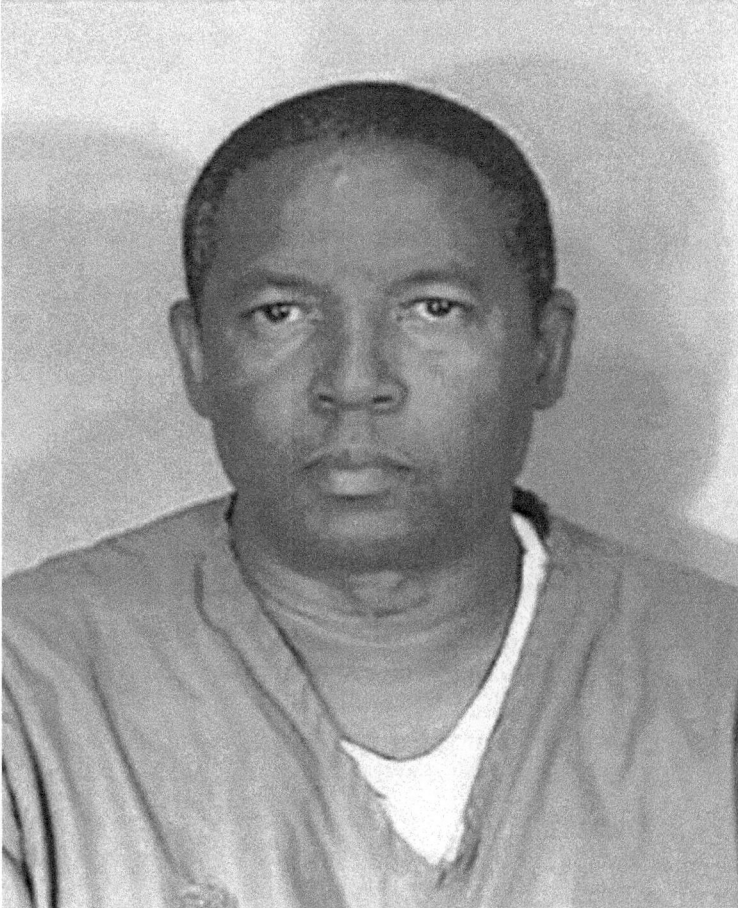

New York State Department of Corrections photo of Nathaniel White in 1993.

With his first victim, Juliana Frank, he claimed, "I had no intention of hurting her. I didn't even know she was pregnant until five days later when I heard it on the news." White also said that until he heard the news, he wasn't even sure he had killed her, thinking that maybe it was all some sort of a terrible dream. When he realized he had actually committed the horrible crime, he panicked—but obviously not enough to stop killing.

"I couldn't help myself," White asserted. "That's why I decided to tell everything. I don't want to do it anymore."

The abandoned house on Harriman Drive where the bodies of Angelina Hopkins and Brenda Whiteside were found near a shed in the backyard.
The house burned down in 2015.
Legoland is currently being built on the land next to Harriman Drive.
Credit: Kazfiel Creative Commons

White's confession made a good story for television, but the simple truth was that if he hadn't been caught when he was, the body count would surely have risen dramatically.

That same day, as the interview was taking place, a judge appointed a defense lawyer, Bernard Brady, for White, whose first act was to immediately stop the interview. While it seemed that telling the world of his guilt guaranteed that White would be put away for life, his constitutional rights now came into question, as became glaringly obvious in an August 6, 1992 letter to the editor of the *New York Times*, from two of the most powerful criminal defense lawyers in the country. Would the unthinkable happen, and would White walk free because *his rights* had been violated?

To the Editor:

As both criminal-defense lawyers and as United States citizens, we were aghast that the authorities in New York's Orange County permitted reporters from WNBC-TV in New York City and The Middletown Times Herald Record to interview Nathaniel White, a suspect in the serial murders of six Hudson Valley women.

During this interview, while Mr. White was in police custody, he confessed to the murders. The police and the prosecution deliberately permitted the interviews to take place, although Mr. White's appointed lawyer had not been informed about them.

We cannot imagine a grosser violation of a criminal suspect's rights. That the crimes attributed to Mr. White are indeed heinous can hardly excuse such callous indifference to his most fundamental constitutional rights. This conduct by the authorities cannot be justified by any claim of law enforcement necessity, as any confession or admissions so obtained could not possibly be introduced against the defendant at his trial.

The only conceivable advantage gained by the prosecution, namely to poison the potential jury pool, is as unconstitutional as permitting the interviews themselves.

Tragically, we have apparently reached the stage where people suspected of the most terrible crimes can be deliberately stripped of the rights that are guaranteed to everyone by both the New York State and Federal constitutions. Once such misconduct is countenanced for the Nathaniel Whites of this world, then the rights of everyone else are dangerously jeopardized.

Had we, as defense lawyers, engaged in such egregious misconduct, we would surely have been confronted with disciplinary charges. The police and the prosecutors who orchestrated the White interviews should be subjected to the sternest of sanctions by their appropriate oversight agencies.

WILLIAM M. KUNSTLER and RONALD L. KUBY, New York, Aug. 6, 1992

Trial

On Thursday, March 11, 1993, the trial of Nathaniel White began in the Orange County Courthouse in Goshen with a jury of eleven men and one woman. Defense attorney Bernard Brady stated that if the judge, Jeffrey G. Berry, was to decide to "knock out the written confession" then "the whole case falls down." There was apparently only "one bloody fingerprint to one murder" [found in Laurette Huggins' home] and some "circumstantial evidence, but without the confession the DA admits they couldn't prove their case." Would the judge allow White's 8-page written confession and the WNBC interview to be entered into evidence? Or would Judge Berry strike the confessions and leave the prosecution stranded?

In his opening statement, DA Phillips said about the six victims, "We will prove the one thing they all had in common was that the last human being they saw on Earth was that man, Nathaniel White. You will hear the guilt from Mr. White's own words...I think it's going to be a lengthy trial. You'll see everything comes together and points the finger at Nathaniel White."

Brady countered by stating that police were "stumped" in the cases of the six murdered and missing women, and so "They leaped at the opportunity to sweep Mr. White off the streets as the first available suspect...there is more to this case than the simple little tale Mr. Phillips told you."

Brady went on to assert that police lied, threatened to arrest Jill Garrison, and coerced White into his confession after 18 hours of interrogation in which he was denied counsel. Initially, Brady had planned on an insanity defense, but White simply came across as too calm, collected, and well-spoken, showing nothing a jury might consider to be in the category of "crazy." The defense's only hope was to demonstrate that White's rights had been violated so as to have his confessions stricken from the record.

After opening remarks, eight witnesses were called to testify that first day, including:

- Christine Klebbe's father, Christopher Garrison, "told the jury that two weeks after his daughter disappeared, White assured him she was alive and well."
- Lorraine Healy and Gregory Rooker described how they found Juliana Frank's mutilated body.
- Two Middletown police sergeants testified that Frank's "face had been slashed and her belly slit open" and that she had been stabbed more than 30 times. One of the officers also said that he saw Huggins' body in her home and that she had also been stabbed more than 30 times.
- Frank's mother, Beverly Tyrian, testified that her daughter was three months pregnant. Outside the courthouse after her testimony, Mrs. Tyrian said, "I'd just like to do to him what he did to my daughter. I swear I would."
- Gary Young described the horror of finding the "bloody corpse" of his friend, Laurette Huggins.

The trial was indeed lengthy, as dozens of witnesses testified over the course of four weeks. But no witness was as riveting as Nathaniel White. At first hoping to keep White off the stand, after Brady's strategy to show how cops violated his client's rights failed, he felt he had no choice.

Jurors later stated that White's testimony was riddled with inconsistencies and his answers seemed "tailored" to try to explain everything with less than credible excuses. For example, White claimed that his bloody fingerprint was in Huggins' home because he was actually the first one to discover her body. Fearing that he would be accused of the crime, he ran away, and for some unknown reason he took the murder weapon with him and then hid it!

Conspiracy was White's main argument—a vast conspiracy of police and victims' families to falsely accuse and convict him. DA Phillips pointed out during a break in the proceedings that according to White, *everyone* involved in this case was lying, *except* White.

Arguably, an even greater impact on the jury than White's personal testimony in court, was his 37-minute television interview. When Brady put his client on the stand, it opened the door for that video to be shown to the jury. Several jurors later commented that White's written confession had been "blunt" and lacked details, and overall wasn't a slam-dunk piece of evidence. However, White's television appearance contained a startling degree of detail, and the way he expressed himself also portrayed a man who, for once in his life, was telling the truth about what he had done.

However, near the end of the trial, Brady attempted to cast some serious doubt by naming one of White's friends and saying that this man could have actually committed all the murders. White had brought Angelina Hopkins and Brenda Whiteside to this man's house on the night they disappeared, and this man also knew some of the other victims. In fact, he had lived on the same street as Adraine Hunter. Was this bombshell enough to plant a seed of reasonable doubt?

On Monday, April 12, the jury was handed the case. While family members waited outside and prayed for quick guilty verdicts, three long hours dragged by with no decision. The jury was sequestered for the night, and the following day at 9am they continued their deliberations. Prosecutors began getting nervous at how long it was taking, and how many pieces of evidence the jury kept requesting. They wondered if defense attorney Brady had succeeded in casting sufficient doubt to free Nathaniel White.

After a full nine and a half hours of deliberations, the jury had finally made its decision. While White appeared calm and unconcerned, as he had throughout the trial, family members were on the edge of their seats. While even one guilty verdict would have been satisfying, everyone wanted justice for *their* loved ones, with a guilty verdict specifically for their daughter, sister, mother, or friend.

Finally, there were the six words that ended so many months of anguish—guilty, guilty, guilty, guilty, guilty, guilty. Nathaniel White was found guilty in all six murders.

While victims' family members cried and laughed and hugged each other and the DA, and some even planned the "biggest party Orange County has ever seen," one victim's father felt no great joy or cause for celebration.

Matthew Whiteside, Brenda's father, said solemnly, "It just don't change a hell of a lot for me. My daughter is still gone."

And how did this newly-convicted serial killer react to the verdicts?

"I'm a victim of injustice," White declared, and went on to say that he had now found his true calling in life, to become a civil rights activist.

"Because I realize at this point that a black man has no rights. *I'm a victim*, OK?"

White: I'm a 'victim' of injustice

Racism, police cited for murder conviction

Poughkeepsie Journal, April 15, 1993

Still maintaining his innocence and insinuating that the true killer was still out there, he further added, "And I don't wish death or violence on anyone, but I believe that when other women's bodies start being found, maybe people will think twice."

"My immediate plan now is to focus all of my attentions into my appeal and to keep in touch with my family and my loved ones and to increase my knowledge of the law," White continued. He said his trial was unfair, and he had been forced into the written confession and tricked to repeat it on WNBC-TV. "If it was a senator's son, they would have suppressed the statements, they would have suppressed the videotape, they would have suppressed it all. But because I'm a nobody and I'm just a little black man and I'm nobody important, then the same rules don't apply to me."

The *Poughkeepsie Journal* reported that, "Poughkeepsie resident Renee Hopkins laughed when she heard about White's diatribe on racial injustice. Five of his six victims were black, including her sister, Angelina.

'If he wants to be a civil rights activist, then I would like to know what rights did those girls have?' "

Sentencing and Punishment

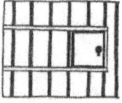

On Wednesday, May 26, 1993, Judge Berry told Nathaniel White, "I am not sentencing you out of anger. Our society deserves to be free from a brutal killer."

As the judge read off the names of White's victims, he stopped at the name of 14-year-old Christine Klebbe to say in front of a stunned courtroom, "Why the little kid?"

"Is that a question?" White replied.

"You don't need to answer me," Judge Berry said. "It's a rhetorical question."

White, who was actually smiling throughout the initial phase of the sentencing proceedings, finally changed his expression as family members began making their statements.

Linda Whiteside, the sister of victim Brenda Whiteside, whom had been bludgeoned to death and dumped in a field, said, as she looked directly at White:

"I wish I could yell. I wish could scream. I wish I could kick. I wish I could hit. I wish I could do to you what you did to my sister and others."

Other family members spoke to how their lives had been changed, and the incredible pain they had to deal with every day. They also produced a petition containing 3,000 signatures urging Judge Berry to pronounce the harshest sentence allowed by law.

Judge Berry did not hesitate to give Nathaniel White 150 years to life for his terrible crimes.

In his statement, White told the courtroom, "I did not kill those people. Every right that the law said I had was violated. The only right that I had that was upheld was my right to trial by jury. A poor black man has no legal rights."

The spectators reacted to his last pronouncement by "hissing."

For all of White's declarations of innocence and claims that he was the victim, he now sits in prison in Elmira, as inmate number 93A4050. He will not be eligible for parole until October of 2137, which guarantees he will never receive his third parole.

Murder Most Foul

Crime Scene

After almost two years of women disappearing from the streets of Poughkeepsie, NY from 1996 to 1998, it was clear that crimes were being committed, but with no bodies and no crime scenes, police had very little to go on. They knew that the women were probably prostitutes with drug addictions, they knew their names, they had their photos and the dates they went missing, but they didn't have one drop of blood or strand of hair or fiber at any location. In other words, they didn't have a clue or a suspect.

Some of the prostitutes in town had complained about one customer in particular, Kendall Francois, a 6' 4" African American who weighed between 350 and 400 pounds. This massive man, known for his poor hygiene (his nickname in school had been "Stinky"), was also known for his proclivity for very rough sex.

As a result of these reports, police began a seven-day surveillance on his home at 99 Fulton Avenue—not far from prestigious Vassar College—in Poughkeepsie in January of 1997, but the house was never searched and Francois faded from their radar. Meanwhile, the disappearances continued and the list of petite, brown-haired, prostitutes-gone-missing was growing longer:

Wendy Meyers, 30, white female, reported missing in October of 1996.

Gina Barone, 29, white female, reported missing by her mother in December of 1996.

Kathleen Hurley, 47, white female, reported missing in January of 1997.

Catherine Marsh, 31, white female, reported missing by her mother in March 1997.

Mary Healey Giaccone, 29, white female, reported missing in November 1997.

Sandra Jean French, 51, white female, reported missing by her daughter in June 1998.

Catina Newmaster, 25, white female, reported missing in August of 1998.

Wendy Meyers

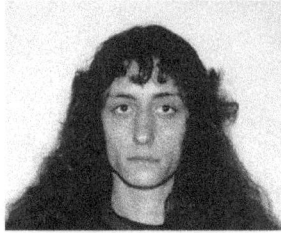

Gina Barone

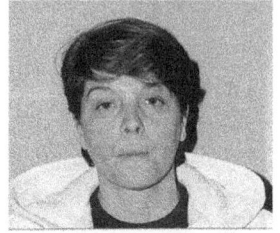

Kathleen Hurley

Catherine Marsh

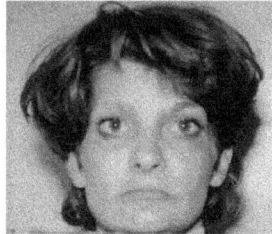

Mary Giaccone

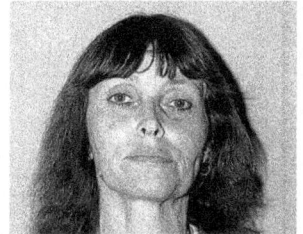

Sandra French

Catina Newmaster

Finally, there was a major break in the case on September 1, 1998. Police Detectives Skip Mannain and Bob McCready went to a gas station with flyers for the Catina Newmaster disappearance. They were informed that a woman, Christine Sala, had just been there and she claimed that she had been assaulted. Racing to find Sala, she told police she knew exactly who had tried to strangle her—Kendall Francois.

Brought in for questioning, Francois, 27, admitted to the murders and was arrested. The next day, armed with a search warrant, police descended on 99 Fulton Avenue; the home this brutal serial killer shared with his parents and sister—the same home where he strangled and drowned prostitutes and hid their bodies. After almost two years with no crime scene, investigators were about to uncover a nightmarish scene unlike any other they would ever encounter in their careers. It was a true house of horrors.

Upon entering the house, they were assaulted by a foul stench beyond description. In fact, the odor was so strong that even outside in the open air the mailman and neighbors had been smelling something awful for years, with some even complaining it made them gag. Inside, there was dirty underwear in the kitchen, rotting food and garbage was strewn about and filled with maggots, and everything was overrun by cockroaches and covered in rodent feces. No one had ever seen such filthy and appalling living conditions. But that was the least of the disgusting scenes to come.

Mold, animal feces, and human decomp covered the filthy contents of the attic. All house photos courtesy of the Town of Poughkeepsie Police Department.

Decaying human bodies were soon discovered in the attic and basement. For those corpses that had sufficiently rotted, Francois had pulled off their skulls and tossed them in a blue kiddie pool in the attic. The decomp was so bad that one investigator stated that the soupy human remains ruined two pairs of his boots. Investigators in white biohazard suits and masks peeled back layers of clothes and blankets to reveal the putrefying corpses and then painstakingly bagged all of the evidence. It was a long, arduous, traumatizing task that none of them would ever forget.

The filth and garbage in the basement where more bodies were hidden.

In the end, all seven missing women's bodies were found. To their surprise, investigators also uncovered an eighth body in the house, that of Audrey Pugliese, 34, from New Rochelle, NY. No one expected to find Pugliese simply because no one had ever reported her missing!

Like many other serial killers, Kendall Francois had chosen his victims from a segment of society that generates little sympathy or regard.

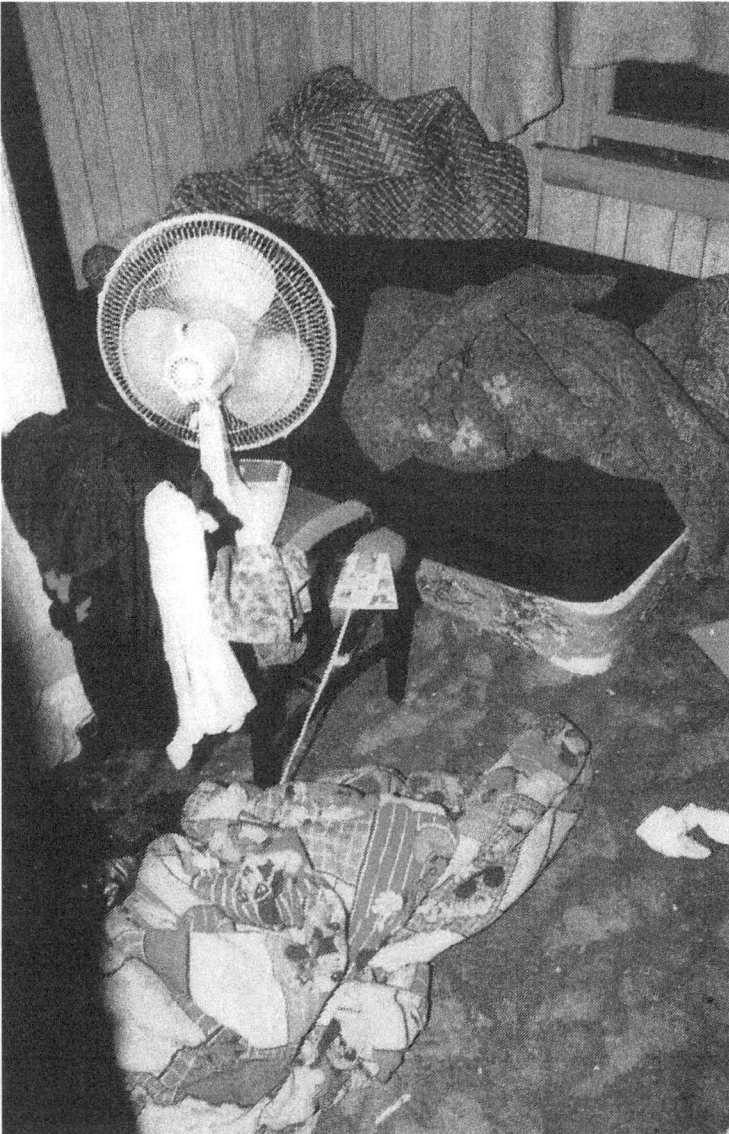

Kendall Francois' bedroom where he killed several women. The blanket hanging over the window is covered in black mold. Note the Mickey Mouse comforter on the floor. When Francois killed Sandra French, he left her body on that comforter while he got dressed and then left to go to school.

Investigation

When Gina Barone first went missing in December of 1996, her mother, Patricia, knew that something bad had happened. Police assumed that a woman such as Gina—a prostitute with a drug habit—had just "gone out of town," even though Patricia kept insisting that her daughter *never* left town.

When she learned that Wendy Meyers had also gone missing two months earlier, Patricia tried to convince the *Poughkeepsie Journal* to run an article alerting people that someone was abducting women. The newspaper had no interest, saying that there was nothing unusual for two women like Meyers and Barone to drop out of sight for a while, and that certainly didn't warrant a story. Patricia told them she was sure that if just one college girl from Vassar had disappeared there would be plenty of newspaper coverage.

Even within the police department, some officers were initially urging their colleagues not to waste manpower on these types of women, who were not exactly the most reliable and responsible citizens. However, when more women started disappearing and it finally became clear that there was a predator on the streets of Poughkeepsie, skeptical law enforcement agencies became believers. They also suddenly realized that every *john* that sought out the city's many prostitutes was now a suspect. As so many men came from far and wide in the Hudson Valley to pay for sex on the streets of the town, the police had a lot of potential suspects.

In the beginning of the police investigation, Kendall Francois was a suspect for a short time, but in hindsight he was arguably not considered as seriously as he should have been; he was under surveillance for only a week, and with no probable cause found during that time, a search warrant was never obtained.

Another missed opportunity came in November of that year, when yet another prostitute and drug addict, Debbie Annan, had gone to the police and told them that she had almost been killed. While standing on the corner of Montgomery and Academy Streets, Kendall Francois drove up and engaged her services. Bringing her to his house, Francois attempted to strangle Annan, but she managed to get away.

Annan was known to police as she had occasionally acted as an informant about drug deals, so she was already a source of information.

However, for whatever reason, the police did not believe her story about Francois trying to kill her and *did nothing*—even though just several months earlier he had been one of their prime suspects! Annan even went to the police a second time to tell them about Francois' homicidal tendencies, but again to no avail.

The Francois house at 99 Fulton Avenue where
many women went in, but never came out alive.

Then on January 18, 1998, police pulled over Francois and asked if he would come to headquarters to answer questions about a rumor that he had threatened a prostitute with a knife. He complied, and even when he was taken to an interrogation room in which there were photos of his victims and his house on the wall, he was not unnerved and calmly denied the charge, saying it wasn't a knife, just a harmless nail file.

Kendall Francois the day of his arrest.

Remarkably, he even let Detective Mannain into his house—where the detective first encountered the inconceivable filth and stench—but Mannain again saw nothing that would call for a search warrant. (Several years later, a reporter said that Francois thought that having Mannain *inside* his house with all of the bodies was the funniest thing.) And when Francois then passed a polygraph examination, police once again had nothing to pin the crimes on him.

The second time Francois was brought to police headquarters was eight months later, when he confessed and all of his victims' bodies were subsequently found in the attic and basement. The initial phase of the investigation was over. Evidence retrieval now took center stage, while other investigators looked into the background of the man the press simply called "The Poughkeepsie Killer."

Francois was born in Poughkeepsie on July 26, 1971, and had grown up in the same home he would later use as his slaughterhouse. At Arlington High School, his large size made him ideal for the school football and wrestling teams. After graduating, he joined the Army in 1990, but was discharged in 1992 for obesity. Beginning in 1993, he went to Dutchess Community College and took classes for several years.

One of the most disturbing things police found out about Francois was that he worked at Arlington Middle School from 1996 to 1997 as a kind of a hall monitor. Some students complained that he was too strict and gave out too many detentions. Teachers were alarmed that he openly acted inappropriately with the female students. In retrospect, their alarm had been more than justified as during the time he was flirting with young students, he was murdering prostitutes.

It was no secret among the prostitutes in town that Kendall Francois was a regular customer, as well as a fellow drug user. "Most of us knew him," said one of the prostitutes. "We did crack together."

Another interesting fact that was discovered was that Kendall Francois also shared something else with the prostitutes—their diseases. In 1995, it was determined that Francois was HIV positive. In a stunning twist, he most likely became infected by Wendy Meyers, his first victim! Had Francois known that Wendy gave him HIV, and had that been part of the rage which led to his murder spree?

Regardless of what was going on in his mind as he stalked and killed his prey, the results of his numerous violent acts were plain for all to see—and smell—at 99 Fulton Avenue. Once all of the grisly evidence had finally been collected, the case against Kendall Francois was then turned over to the court system.

Trial

Initially indicted for the murder of Catina Newmaster on September 4, 1998, Francois actually pleaded not guilty, even though he had previously confessed to the murders. On October 13, an avalanche of charges fell upon The Poughkeepsie Killer to the tune of eight counts of first degree murder, eight counts of second degree murder, as well as attempted assault.

Faced with the death penalty if convicted by a jury of the first degree murder charges, some legal maneuvering took place by Francois' lawyers. Unfortunately, simply catching a murderer is not the end of the story. The legal system in the United States is both a blessing and a curse, as in an effort to protect the innocent, the guilty may worm their way out of a conviction, or at least the punishment his crime deserves. Justice is not only blind; sometimes it is morally wrong.

How could someone who murdered eight women—and who admitted he would have just kept killing if he hadn't been caught—avoid the death penalty? A legal loophole, and one large enough to drive a 6' 4", 350-pound serial killer through.

When Francois was arraigned in court for his indictment on October 8, 1998, the death penalty clock started to tick. From that day, the District Attorney had 120 days in which to decide whether or not to serve a notice of intent to seek the death penalty in this case. However, before DA William Grady could file the death penalty notice, Francois' lawyers made an unscheduled appearance at the Dutchess County Court on December 23 to suddenly offer a plea of guilty to the entire indictment.

In technical terms, in the case of Haynes v. Tomei, "avoidance of the maximum penalty for conviction of the capital offense could only be assured to defendants who plead guilty rather than assert innocence and go to trial before a jury." In simple language, by rushing to the courthouse and pleading guilty before Grady could declare his intention to seek the death penalty, Francois would escape the fate he had dealt to those eight women, and he'd be able to live out the remainder of his natural life.

It was an outrage, and one that the DA's office would fight. The ensuing battle was something of a legal back and forth tennis match, with Francois' life hanging in the balance. The County Court refused to accept the guilty plea under those circumstances. Francois' lawyers countered by filing a petition with the Appellate Division to compel the court to accept the plea. The Appellate Division dismissed the petition, declaring that the petitioner "failed to demonstrate a clear legal right to the relief sought" (263 AD2d 483). Francois' lawyers appealed that ruling to the Court of

Appeals on March 28, 2000. On May 18, 2000, the Court of Appeals ruled and upheld the Appellate decision, stating:

"The legislative scheme does not support the theory that a person indicted for capital murder has an unqualified right, by pleading guilty to the indictment, to thwart the statutory authority of a District Attorney to make a fully deliberative decision whether to seek the death penalty, within the 120-day period after arraignment prescribed by CPL 250.40(2)."

The Court of Appeals accurately summed it up by saying that to permit this guilty plea would encourage others in a race to the courthouse between the DA and the defense in order to be first. This wise decision meant that Francois would indeed go to trial and face the death penalty if convicted on the charges of first degree murder.

However, despite that legal victory, in June of 2000, DA Grady actually *did* accept the guilty plea after all! According to the *New York Times*: *Mr. Grady said today that he still favored execution, but that he allowed Mr. Francois to plead guilty chiefly because some victims' relatives did not want details of the crimes made public at a trial. "Many of the families do not want their children and grandchildren needlessly exposed," he said. Mr. Grady added that although he believes that Mr. Francois was not insane at the time, the defendant does have clear psychological problems that might lead a jury to decide against the death penalty. Theoretically, that would make it possible for Mr. Francois to be paroled someday.*

Was justice ultimately served? Justice, like beauty, is often in the eye of the beholder, but then again, justice is blind.

SPECIAL REPORT

Francois pleads guilty to killing eight women

Poughkeepsie Journal headline, June 22, 2000

Punishment and Aftermath

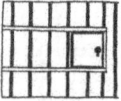

After all of the legal wrangling about whether or not Francois' guilty plea could be accepted, the stage was finally set for sentencing. On August 11, 2000, serial killer Kendall Francois was sentenced to life in prison—with no possibility of parole. He began serving his time at the Attica Correctional Facility.

POUGHKEEPSIE JOURNAL   THURSDAY, JUNE 22, 2000

Francois will spend life behind bars

Francois escaped a long lifetime of incarceration, however, when he died at 6:15pm on September 11, 2014, at the age of only 43 at the Wende Correctional Facility's Regional Medical Unit in Alden, New York. Two years previously, a cancerous tumor had been found in his groin, and he underwent treatment including chemotherapy. However, as his death was only listed as the result of "natural causes," it would be a unique form of justice if the HIV he had contracted from the first woman he killed, Wendy Meyers, was what ultimately killed him.

"I would say that he died too soon and didn't suffer long enough, but the world's a better place without people like him," then-retired Detective Mannain stated, after learning of Francois' death.

And with that, The Poughkeepsie Killer entered the footnotes of history and joined the frighteningly long ranks of the serial killers we can never truly understand, and can only pray that we can swiftly identify and stop them—by whatever means necessary.

Letters from a Monster

"It's a hard lesson to learn that one of the foundations upon which I based my life is false. Women are no better than men."

These words were written in neat script by Kendall Francois in a letter he wrote while he was incarcerated in Attica prison. In another bizarre twist in this case, we can actually peer into his twisted mind and personality thanks to letters he exchanged for years with a young woman.

The odd friendship began in 1998 with 17-year-old Kristina Sharpe, when they were both being held in the Dutchess County Jail. Sharpe was being held on assault charges for attacking another woman with a knife. She was convicted, but only sentenced to probation.

Like something out of a Hollywood script, during her time in jail, she started talking to Francois in the cell below hers through the ventilation system. That led to an exchange of letters, which continued for years. When Francois died in 2014, Sharpe came forward and showed the letters to the *Poughkeepsie Journal,* revealing some remarkable information.

"If you want to know something about me," he wrote, "I was once filled with a darkness so complete I'm not even sure it was part of me. It didn't feel like it. To this day there are times that I have to remind myself that it was the same hands that are now writing to you that ended so many lives. I don't feel like a killer most of the time."

Ironically, Francois would end his letters with "God Bless!" and "Your Friend, Kendall."

He admitted that there was a "darkness in my soul and a rage in my heart," and that while he truly believed all of the women he killed deserved to die, they did not deserve to die by his hands. Such revelations would be small consolation to the relatives of the victims, such as Marguerite Marsh, the mother of Catherine Marsh, the fourth woman he murdered. In 2008, she actually found the courage to see Francois in prison.

"He didn't really say that he was sorry for what he had done," Marguerite said. "I guess that was the most disturbing part of the visit. I had hoped he would apologize."

In fact, he was never sorry for what he did, and told a lawyer in a letter that he only did one thing wrong.

"Well, what I did wrong was confess. I should have never confessed. If I had not confessed, they never would have been able to pin it on me."

The Sharpe letters also state mundane things about Francois' "boring" life in prison, where most of his time was spent watching television and reading the Bible. He was hungry for news about Poughkeepsie, and there was some recognition of the fact that he was in prison by his own doing, but there were no expressions of deep remorse for his actions.

When diagnosed with cancer in 2012, he wrote:

"I never thought it would happen, but it could be that I must face the fact that I have more years behind me than ahead at this point in my life."

Too bad he was never sorry for all of the years he stole from those eight women, or the countless years of suffering that he caused their families.

A February 10, 2014 photo of Francois in prison. He died seven months later. New York State Department of Corrections photo.

Death Mask

Crime Scene

While hiking through the woods near Buckberg Mountain Road in Tomkins Cove, N.Y. on Sunday, March 17, 1985, five people came across a sight they would never forget. Inside a cramped, 18th-century stone smokehouse was the body of man—or what was left of him.

Almost all of the man's flesh had been burned or eaten by animals. "From the cheek bones down the body was a total skeleton," stated Rockland County Medical Examiner Dr. Frederick Zugibe.

The smokehouse where the remains were found.
Photos courtesy of the Rockland County Sheriff's Office, BCI.

Despite the horrific sight, arguably the most shocking aspect of the scene was the black leather mask which covered the victim's entire head. There were openings for the eyes and nose, but a heavy zipper was closed shut across the mouth. The mask was loosely laced in the back, where two bullets had been fired at point blank range, no doubt killing the victim instantly.

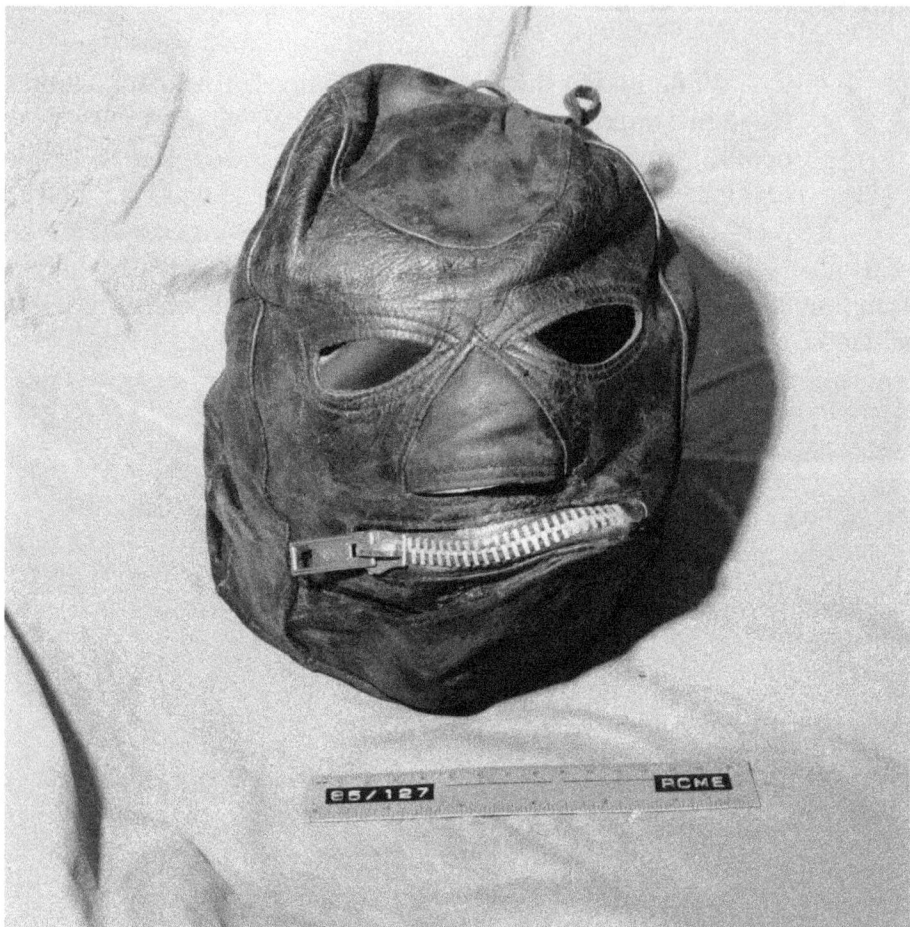

The leather death mask at the time of the autopsy.

In an odd twist, the bizarre bondage mask did serve a useful purpose when identifying the mystery corpse, as it had prevented the scavenging animals from eating all of the man's face. Enough of the victim's features had been preserved so he could be identified as the missing 26-year-old Norwegian student and model, Eigil Dag Vesti, who had been attending the Fashion Institute of Technology in New York City. Vesti had last been seen alive on February 22, when two friends (one of whom was the daughter of famed actor Richard Burton) dropped him off at his apartment on West 26th Street at 1:30am.

How Eigil Vesti ended up 40 miles to the north, murdered and burned in a smokehouse, was the frightening question local residents, and of course, law enforcement, were asking.

Investigation

Eigil Dag Vesti

The death mask also gave police a vital clue as to where to start looking for suspects, as NYPD Detective Robert Intartaglio said such masks were used by the "fringes of the sado-masochistic homosexual community."

Further insight was provided by Stony Point Police Chief Stephen Scurti, who pointed out that the smokehouse where Vesti's remains were found could only be accessed by climbing down an embankment. "You don't happen upon it by chance. Someone had to know it was here."

The smokehouse was part of the 2.5 acre property at 100 Buckberg Mountain Road, which also contained a pre-Revolutionary War-era house. It was owned by United Nations executive John LeGeros, who worked on projects to aid third world countries. He and his wife, Raquel, lived in New York City and only used the place as a summer home. They hardly seemed to be the type to commit such a horrific murder, but another member of the family quickly surfaced to the top of the suspect list.

Their son, Bernard LeGeros, was 22, and worked in Manhattan at the Andrew Crispo Art Gallery at 47 East 57th Street. Soon after the news of the discovery of the body began to spread through the media, Bernard contacted the police to offer his theories as to the grisly slaying.

Bernard LeGeros was not exactly a tough nut to crack. All of his attempts to construct theories on the case quickly crumbled into a shocking confession; he was promptly arrested, and was arraigned on

Thursday, March 21, at the Stony Point Town Court on second-degree murder charges. But that didn't mean the case was closed. According to LeGeros, there had been another man involved in the violent sex games and subsequent brutal murder.

The LeGeros house overlooking the Hudson River.

Bernard LeGeros

On the night that Vesti had gone missing, LeGeros stated that he and his boss, Andrew Crispo, had driven Vesti to the Tomkins Cove estate in a 1974 Oldsmobile station wagon. What ensued was "several hours of master-slave sadomasochistic sexual activity" as the March 23 edition of the local paper, *The Journal News*, reported.

Then between 4 and 5am, they took Vesti, who was naked, and wearing only the mask, out into the cold February night and brought him to the smokehouse. Making Vesti drop to his knees, LeGeros then stood over him with a rifle and shot him twice in the back of the head. LeGeros and Crispo then tried to burn the body, with limited success. They later returned to try to burn the body again, and finally just left Vesti's corpse to the scavenging animals.

1974 Oldsmobile station wagon used to drive Vesti to the LeGeros house.

LeGeros told authorities everything, even where to find the murder weapon, an AR-7, .22 caliber rifle—in Crispo's art gallery—and it was right where he said it would be. His information also led police to find Vesti's clothing, which had been tossed along the Palisades Parkway in New Jersey, as well as "sex paraphernalia" used that night. It seemed to be an open and shut case against the two men who tortured and murdered Eigil Vesti, except for one detail. Whereas LeGeros spilled every lurid detail to police, as well as also confessing to his brother and a friend, Crispo wasn't talking.

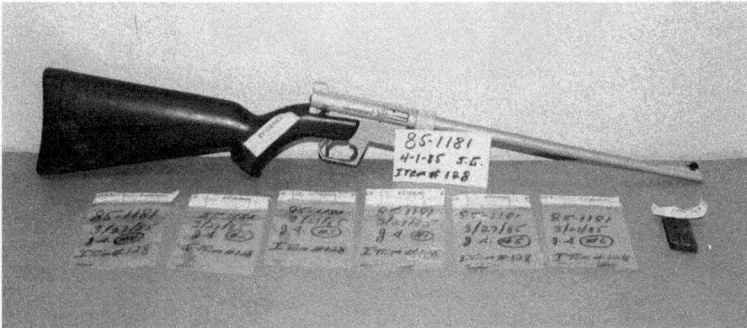

The murder weapon found at Crispo's gallery in Manhattan.

Trial

"We have therein clubs that exist in New York City and parts of Greenwich Village, a Sodom and Gomorrah, where people are interested in S&M and B&D, outlandish sexual activities. We are going to take you through the sewers and mud and slush that this case has its scenes."

This was part of one of the opening statements (taken verbatim) in the trial of Bernard LeGeros held in the New City courthouse in fall of 1985, but it was not made by the prosecutor, District Attorney Kenneth Gribetz. That statement was actually made by 82-year-old Murray Sprung, the *defense* attorney representing LeGeros!

Murray, whom *The Journal News* described as looking like an "Old Testament prophet in a blue suit," realized that his client's confession had left no doubt in anyone's mind that LeGeros had pulled the trigger, so he had to take a different tack by putting all the dirty little secrets out on the table, and then attempting to redirect the blame.

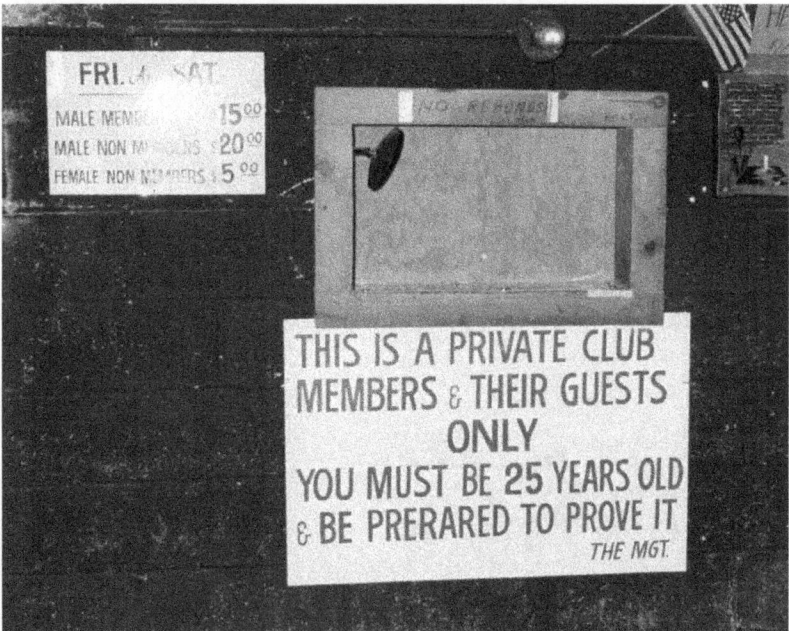

Entrance to the Hellfire Club in Manhattan, where Crispo met Vesti.

Some of the sex apparatus at the Hellfire.

"Bernard LeGeros is innocent by reason of mental defect," Sprung stated.

Cocaine had clouded LeGeros' mind, Sprung asserted, and he had become a cocaine addict because of Andrew Crispo, who bought the drug on a daily basis. Crispo then "ensnared" his young employee and led him into "deviant behavior" such as the numerous sadomasochistic, homosexual acts they enjoyed with men they picked up from the clubs. The murder was Crispo's idea, he ordered LeGeros to shoot Vesti, and even directed him to go to the police to present the rehearsed theories on the crime. Crispo was the puppet master and LeGeros was just another helpless victim every step of the way, or so Sprung wanted the jury to believe.

Andrew Crispo

The only problem was that Crispo still wasn't talking.

Andrew Crispo had stated that he would only testify if he was granted full immunity, to which Gribetz told a colleague, "I wouldn't immunize him if hell froze over." Subpoenaed by the defense, Crispo was brought to a second-floor courtroom in front of Judge Meehan, and away from the jury. When Crispo exercised his constitutional right against self-incrimination for every question asked of him—including something as basic as to whether he knew LeGeros—the judge decided it was pointless to put him on the stand. With not one word from Crispo, and no other direct evidence found to place him at the scene of the murder, LeGeros was on his own, and the jury had only one direction in which to point the bloody finger of guilt.

After 14 days of testimony and only two and a half hours of deliberation, on September 26, Bernard LeGeros was found guilty of the murder of Eigil Dag Vesti, and Judge Meehan would later give him the maximum sentence of 25 years to life.

Remarkably, Andrew Crispo was *never charged* in the murder. Under New York law, LeGeros' testimony would not be admissible. As there were no witnesses to the actual crime and no evidence was ever found placing Crispo at the crime scene, Gribetz decided not to prosecute. If we are to believe LeGeros' twisted tale of the murder, and there is no compelling reason not to on this point, then a guilty man walked free.

A photo of Vesti and a copy of his missing poster were found in Crispo's gallery.

Punishment and Aftermath

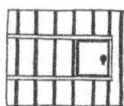

After serving 25 years in the Clinton Correctional Facility, also known as Dannemora, Bernard LeGeros was eligible for parole in March of 2010. His parole was denied, as has every other attempt as of the writing of this book in 2018. However, despite being incarcerated, LeGeros still managed to make some headlines over the years.

For example, in 2001, after reading all about LeGeros' sadomasochistic practices and ruthless murder, Jeanne Bissonnette flew from Washington state to New York to meet him, and two hours later she proposed marriage! They were married at the prison, and Bissonnette stated that she hoped they would "one day bond on the molecular level by having a baby."

Her wish came true, as on one of their conjugal visits in a prison trailer, she became pregnant. However, after the birth of their son, a custody battle soon ensued. LeGeros wanted his parents to have custody of the boy, while Bissonnette demanded full custody. Reality is stranger than fiction!

Bernard LeGeros is now in Attica prison, awaiting his next parole hearing.

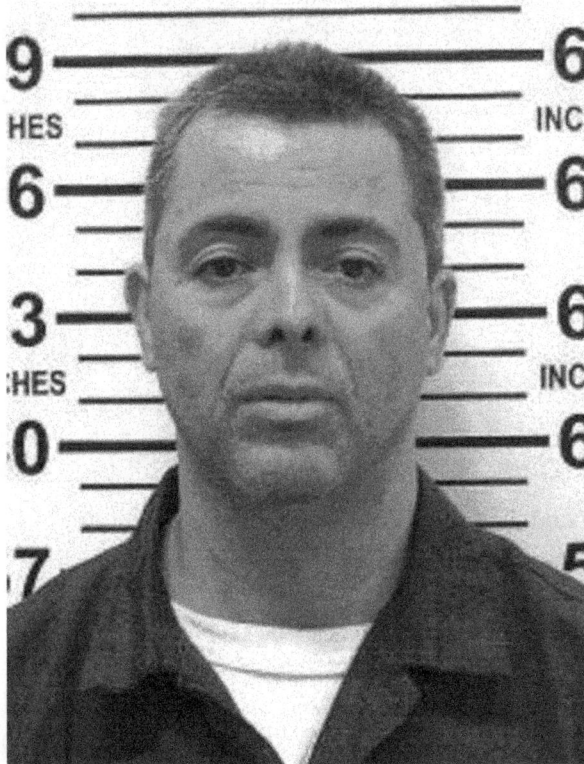

NYS Department of Corrections photo of an older LeGeros in prison.

Despite eluding justice in the Vesti case, Andrew Crispo was arrested and brought to trial in 1988 for the kidnapping and assault of another young art student, Robert Kasanof. However, the jury was not convinced a crime had been committed, and concluded that "by objective facts, that whatever happened was of a voluntary, social nature." In other words, they believed that Kasanof willingly submitted to Crispo's abuse. Once again, Andrew Crispo was free man.

While it seems that you can get away with all sorts of crimes in this country, including murder, you cannot escape the almighty Internal Revenue Service. Accused of owing the IRS $8 million, Crispo finally did plead guilty to something—tax evasion—and was sentenced to seven years.

However, after serving less than three years, Crispo was released in July of 1989, and was again living comfortably in his Southampton mansion. Oddly, just one week later, his mansion blew to pieces in a huge explosion. Given his track record, it was suspected that Crispo was to blame in order to collect the insurance. Nonetheless, in 1991, the Long Island Lighting Company accepted responsibility for the explosion, which apparently had been caused by a gas leak. A jury then awarded Crispo $8.6 million in damages.

Crispo then opened another art gallery for a short time. Over the ensuing years, he was spotted on occasion at restaurants in the city, but overall, he managed to maintain a low profile and avoid any further arrests and trials.

When asked what he thought about his former boss and alleged partner in crime, LeGeros stated, "He belongs in hell. The only thing is that he would enjoy it."

This whip was one of the items found along the Palisades Interstate Parkway that were disposed of after the murder on the drive back to Manhattan.

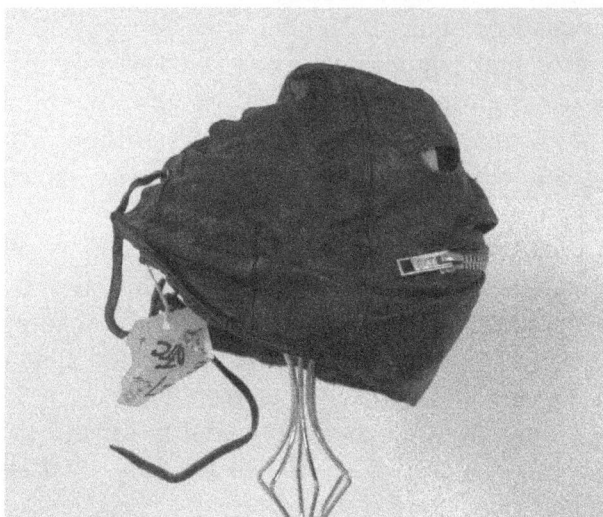

The death mask is on display (but not for public viewing)
at the Rockland County Sheriff's Office in New City, NY.
Side view, above. Back view, below.

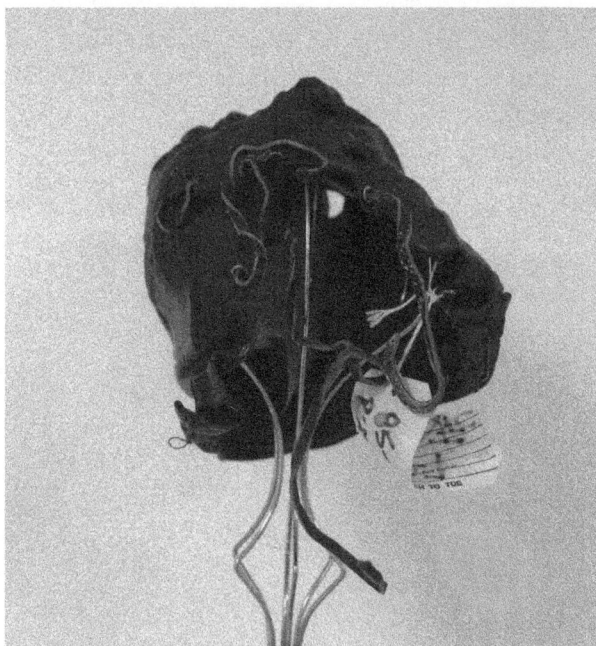

Toy Tomahawk

Crime Scene

Around noon on October 6, 2004, Timothy Gray's neighbor on Elsmere Avenue in Delmar, New York, found his girlfriend's dog wandering on the street. The neighbor went to number 95A to return the dog, and found Tim unconscious in the backyard in a pool of blood. There were numerous wounds on his head and face and the 28-year-old was barely clinging to life.

Timothy Gray's house.
Google Maps image.

The blood spatter pattern clearly showed that there had been an awful struggle and that Tim had been repeatedly and brutally struck with some sort of a weapon. When police questioned the neighbors, one had thought there had been a loud argument and a scream around 10:15pm the night before. If that was the time of the attack, it meant that Gray had been viciously bludgeoned, beaten, and unconscious for almost 14 hours—precious time without crucial medical attention.

Tim's live-in girlfriend, Jessica Domery, had been out of town for work, so no one was there on that cold night to help the poor young man with the severely fractured face and skull. There was also trauma to his torso from being repeatedly kicked when he was down on the ground, and then left for dead. The question for police was: who could have done such a terrible thing to him? At the Albany hospital where he was brought, the other question became: could anyone help Timothy Gray?

Investigation

The following day, October 7, police Detectives Charles Rudolph and Christopher Bowdish were waiting in the Albany University parking lot by the car of Domery's former boyfriend, 22-year-old student, Erick Westervelt of 659 Salvia Lane, Guilderland—who was studying history and wanted to be a police officer. They asked him to come to Delmar for questioning, as Gray's friends had said that Westervelt was very angry and jealous when Domery had dumped him to return to her former boyfriend, Tim Gray, and that Westervelt had been harassing them both with phone calls.

Westervelt voluntarily went to Delmar, where he was questioned for almost six hours, steadfastly denying that he had assaulted Gray or had been calling and harassing anyone. He claimed he had been home the entire night of the attack, and his parents could verify that. He also said the last time he had seen Gray was in June, when he went to the house to see Domery just a week after their breakup. Westervelt claimed that Gray rushed out and started pushing him, and he shoved back. However, the confrontation did not escalate past a brief scuffle, and Westervelt simply left. That was his story, and he volunteered to return the next day to take a polygraph to prove he was telling the truth.

On October 8, Erick Westervelt was undergoing the polygraph examination when he stopped the test and declared, "I did it." He confessed to punching and kicking Gray in the face and body, as well as striking him with a bizarre choice of weapon—a toy; a wooden, souvenir tomahawk! His confession was videotaped and he drew a detailed map of the crime scene, showing not only where Gray's body was lying by the picnic table and what direction he was facing, but also where the wounds were located on his body. Westervelt was placed under arrest for assault and attempted murder.

On October 10, Timothy Gray—who had been in a coma and on life support—died of his injuries. The charges were upgraded to second degree murder and Westervelt immediately wanted to recant his confession.

Although police did find searches on Westervelt's computer for "murder," they did not find any evidence to link him to the crime scene, and the murder weapon was never found. Westervelt's confession and his motive, jealousy, would have to suffice. It would be up to the jury to decide whether Erick Westervelt was a "gentle, peace-loving" student who had moved on from the breakup with his girlfriend, as his friends and family claimed, or had he remained obsessed with Domery and murdered his rival in a jealous rage with a toy tomahawk?

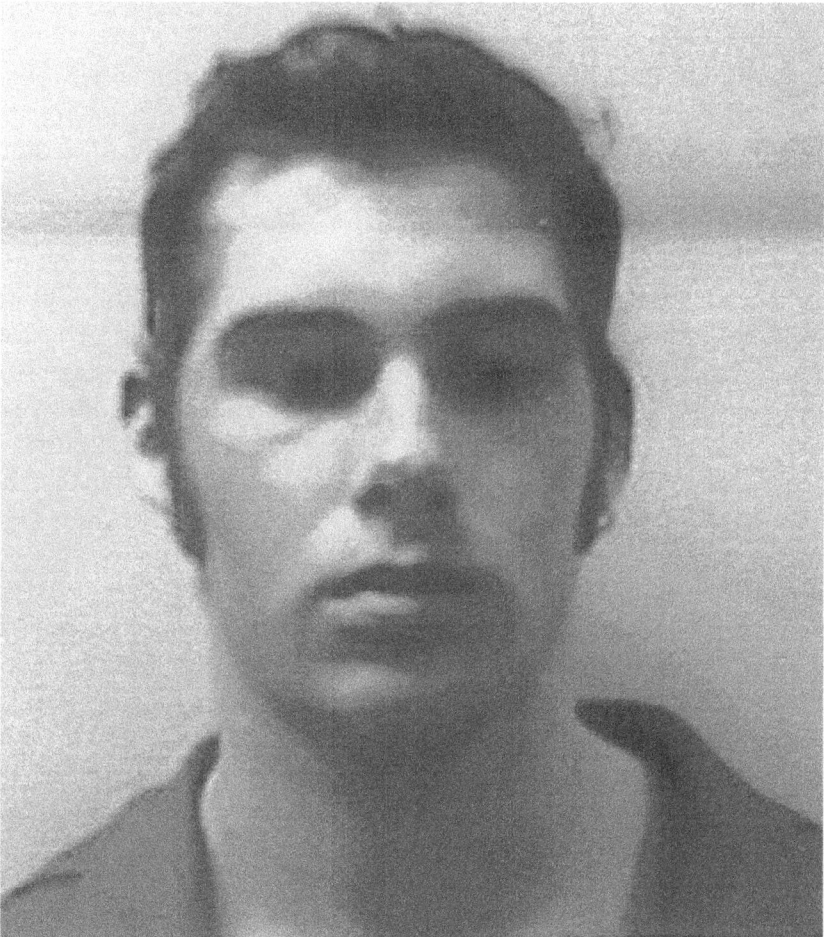

Police handout of Erick Westervelt.

Trial

After Westervelt's arrest, newspapers had a field day calling him a "hatchet murderer," or even an "ax murderer." While the alleged weapon was neither a hatchet nor an ax, these choices of words certainly sounded more evil and deadly. Ultimately, though, it didn't matter whether the weapon was a toy or something else—Timothy Gray had been beaten to death, and it was now up to a jury to decide who had wielded that weapon.

During the trial at the Albany County Courthouse, which began on June 20, 2005, about fifteen of Timothy Gray's friends and family members listened intently to every word, while about eight of Westervelt's friends and family sat on the other side of the courtroom, following the proceedings with equally rapt attention.

Mark Sacco and Kent Sprotberry, Westervelt's attorneys, made their case on the facts that no blood had been found on their client's clothes or in his car, no murder weapon had been precisely identified or recovered, and there were no witnesses to place Westervelt at Gray's house the night of the attack. Both of Westervelt's parents took the stand and swore that their son had been at home that night—as late as midnight—thus establishing an alibi. Westervelt also took the stand to state that he had been at home all night, and that he had gotten over his breakup with Domery, so he had no reason to kill Gray.

The prosecution, led by Assistant District Attorney David Rossi, had only two main components of this case, but they were both very powerful things—motive and a confession. The motive was obvious, he claimed, that Westervelt was a jealous, jilted lover, filled with hatred for his rival. Then there were Westervelt's own words in his confession, which he had written and signed, and which had also been videotaped. Seeing and hearing Westervelt describe in detail how he attacked Timothy Gray, and left him bleeding on the ground, was extremely compelling to the members of the jury.

Sacco claimed that it was a false confession because it had been coerced by the police who had fed him all the details of the case, but the jury saw no coercion. They saw an angry young man venting his rage on the person who had stolen away the love his life.

On June 29, twenty-four hours after the case had gone to the jury, they announced their verdict—guilty of second degree murder. And the Appellate Court would later deny Westervelt's request for a second trial.

Sentencing, Punishment, and Aftermath

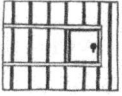

On August 25, 2005, Supreme Court Judge Joseph Teresi sentenced Erick Westervelt to the maximum term of 25 years to life.

"Your acts were cold, calculated, and inhuman and violent," Teresi told Westervelt.

Before the sentence was announced, Timothy Gray's sister, Jennifer, had made a statement to the court, in which she said that "Tim was extremely loyal...He loved unconditionally...He had a smile that would melt your heart."

Jennifer also described the shock and horror of receiving that awful phone call on October 6, 2004, when she learned that her brother had been rushed to the hospital, and she rushed to see him.

"I will never, ever forget what I saw," she said, and then went on to describe seeing her brother with wounds that were "gruesome," in a coma in intensive care with "strips holding his skull together."

"It still feels like yesterday," she added "Sometimes it's hard to even get out of bed...The pain you feel never goes away..."

Media coverage on such homicide cases often focuses so intently on the murderers, that the suffering of the families—of everyone involved—is often overlooked. While Gray's loved ones fought to cope with their loss, Westervelt's loved ones also had to struggle with the tragedy of their son going to prison, perhaps for the remainder of his life. The repercussions of such a heinous crime reverberate through so many people, and across great distances and time.

And it is time which Erick Westervelt now has plenty of, as he sits in the castle-like fortress of the Eastern Correctional Facility in Napanoch, New York. He still maintains his innocence, and a Facebook page called *Free Erick Westervelt* still has regular updates for what his supporters hope will someday lead to a reversal of what they believe is a miscarriage of justice. In 2017, Westervelt's case was featured in an episode of *Reasonable Doubt* on the Investigation Discovery channel. His mother,

Wendy, who steadfastly denies her son's guilt, had hoped the show's investigators would find something to help exonerate him, but they did not.

Westervelt's first parole hearing will not be until June of 2029, with the earliest possible release date of October of 2029. If innocent, that's a very long time to remain behind bars. If guilty, it's not nearly long enough.

Finally, if the reader is on the fence about this case, since it revolved around Erick Westervelt's own spoken and written words, consider this:

After his conviction, in a letter Westervelt wrote to Jessica Domery, he told her how much he missed her, how he never stopped loving her, and how much she had broken his heart. He also added, "I didn't mean to hurt Tim as bad as I did."

***

Additional information from Westervelt's appeal, which was denied:

State of New York
Supreme Court, Appellate Division
Third Judicial Department
Decided and Entered: January 3, 2008 101092

THE PEOPLE OF THE STATE OF
NEW YORK, Respondent,

v

ERICK WESTERVELT, Appellant.

On October 8, 2004, defendant was administered his Miranda rights and then began a polygraph examination, which he terminated part way into the process. According to Bowdish and Rudolph, shortly thereafter he told them, "I did it." While still at the Albany police station, Miranda rights were reread to defendant and he then gave a detailed written statement in which, among other things, he admitted punching Gray, kicking him in the face, striking him in the head and face with a wooden replica hatchet, and leaving a note written in Italian (which he had made using a translation Web site on a computer in a public library) in an effort to detract suspicion. Such a note had been discovered at the premises.

The Forgotten Mass Murderer

Crime Scene

Late in the morning of Thursday, July 26, 1979, Claudine Eggers, 78, was still in bed in her mobile home on Sinpatch Road, in Wassaic, New York. Claudine was a lonely, yet "strong willed" woman, who liked to remain active. She had spent a career helping mentally handicapped children, but had to accept mandatory retirement from her job at age 70. Normally, she would be up and about, but not this morning.

Claudine Eggers was still in bed because she had been stabbed 35 times.

Investigation

On Friday morning, July 27, Claudine's family, friends, and police did not yet know she had been murdered, but that was about to change. A lot of things were about to change.

Joseph Fischer, Claudine's 55-year-old husband of a little less than a year, walked into the 24th Precinct in Manhattan at 8:30am with a can of beer in his hand and announced he had something to confess. At first, the officer thought that this was just another crazy person wanting some attention, but Fischer immediately had the officer's complete attention.

Fischer announced that he had killed his wife in their home the day before. That was nothing, though, compared to the next bombshell. The unassuming-looking man then said he had murdered over 20 people from Maine to California in a coast-to-coast killing spree over the past 13 months.

It was hard to believe, but when police in Dutchess County did indeed find Claudine Eggers' bloody body at about 10am, they began alerting all of the other law enforcement agencies across the country where Fischer said he had killed his many victims. Adding more credibility to his story, police also discovered that Fischer was out on parole—for murder.

How had a 78-year-old woman gotten involved with a 55-year-old convicted murderer? Claudine's family explained that because she was lonely, she had taken part in a pen pal program with prisoners. Fischer apparently wrote all the right things to her, and when he was released on June 27, 1978, they met and decided to get married in August—against the strong protestations and warnings of her family. Even when Fischer immediately began disappearing for months at a time, Claudine was still devoted to him and gave him large sums of money.

"It didn't make any difference. He could do no wrong," Claudine's son later said.

The *Poughkeepsie Journal*, and many other newspapers across the country, followed the Fischer story with great fascination.

However, when examining the life of Joseph Fischer, it became glaringly obvious that he did nothing *but* wrong things.

Born in 1923 in New Jersey, his father was a construction worker and his mother was a prostitute who worked out of their home.

"I guess what really helped me hate the woman was that she didn't care if me or my brothers were home when she brought her customers in," Fischer related, saying that he often watched his mother perform all manner of sex acts on the strangers.

When he expressed his anger at her behavior, he would be beaten.

"I would have killed her ten times over, but I really believe it would have broken my father's heart."

After he was in custody, he even told reporters that his mother "was a whore. If I could dig her up, I would make soup out of her and pee her out."

Fischer even claimed that his mother tried to seduce him when he was 13. It is not surprising, then, that many of the women he killed were prostitutes, or women who looked like his mother. He was, in his twisted mind, indeed killing his mother over and over again.

Catholic school did not go well for the troubled youth, and after robbing a church, he wound up in reform school. After his release in 1938, in order to escape his unbearable home life, he lied about his age so he could join the Merchant Marines at age 15. He soon deserted, but no disciplinary actions were taken when authorities discovered his true age.

After Pearl Harbor, Fischer legitimately joined the Marine Corps. By now, he was an alcoholic (eventually drinking two quarts of Canadian Club Whisky a day) with a huge chip on his shoulder. He actually enjoyed the hellish combat on Guadalcanal, Kwajalein, and Iwo Jima. He even got to kill civilians in China after the Japanese surrendered. While many service men were traumatized by the horrors of World War II, Fischer came away from his experiences realizing that "killing felt too good to stop."

The post-war years were marked by prison and mental institutions for crimes such as severely beating a soldier for five dollars in Branch Brook Park in Essex County, New Jersey. For that crime he was sent to prison until his parole on December 14, 1953.

Fischer went back to Essex County, and less than two weeks after getting out of prison, he met 16-year-old Harry Powell, Jr. on a bus. The two were then walking across Hendricks Field Golf Course where Fischer tied the boy's hands and feet and then repeatedly beat him with a rock, crushing Powell's skull. A couple of days later, Fischer walked into the local police station to confess to the murder and tell them where they could find the body. Sentenced to life in prison for the senseless, brutal murder, it seemed as though Joseph Fischer would never hurt anyone else again.

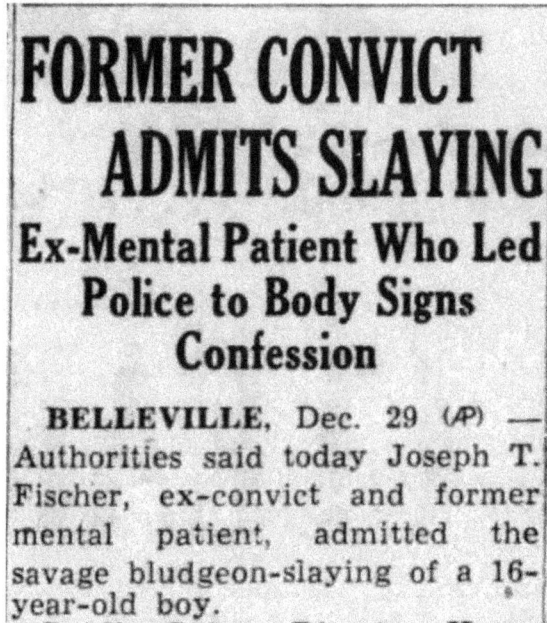

FORMER CONVICT ADMITS SLAYING

Ex-Mental Patient Who Led Police to Body Signs Confession

BELLEVILLE, Dec. 29 (AP) — Authorities said today Joseph T. Fischer, ex-convict and former mental patient, admitted the savage bludgeon-slaying of a 16-year-old boy.

Headline from the *Central New Jersey Home News*, December 29, 1953

Fischer actually escaped from prison after many years, but was recaptured. Twenty-five years into his life sentence in 1978, he was transferred to the Trenton State Psychiatric Hospital. Then the unthinkable occurred—he was granted parole! The conditions of the parole required that he remain under close supervision, but Fischer was soon in the wind, and would not be heard of again until he walked into the 24th Precinct to announce his astonishing body count.

Fischer would later tell one of the investigators that he had decided to go on the country-wide killing spree because he wanted to "top" the kill total of someone he knew in the psychiatric hospital. That other man, Howard Unruh, had opened fire on 16 people in East Camden, NJ in 1949,

84

killing 13 of them. Fischer alleged that this act was what "inspired" him to go on to kill so many people, but it is doubtful he needed any prompting.

Investigators were able to tie Fischer to many of alleged killings using travel receipts that put him at the scenes of the crimes, while others seemed doubtful, or a little hazy. But then again, anyone drinking two quarts of alcohol a day probably doesn't have the sharpest memory.

The murder list was remarkable—two prostitutes in Connecticut he claimed tried to rob him, a man he met at the Salvation Army in California and stabbed to death in a hotel room in Flagstaff, Arizona, and three derelicts in the Bowery in Manhattan.

"I stabbed the guys in the Bowery after they got their (welfare) checks. I either stabbed or choked the woman, I don't remember which."

Then there was Oregon, "somewhere up near Bend, up in the woods. I was drunk and stumbled on this man sleeping in one of them bags. There was a gun lying there and I picked it up and shot him. I guess I just said the hell with it, I'd killed so many already, what did one more matter?"

Also on his list was Betty Jo Gibson of Moore, Oklahoma, whom he met at a dance at a hospital where he "drying out from the two quarts of liquor" he drank every day. On April 18, 1978, Fischer went to a yard sale at Gibson's house. The next day, he bludgeoned her to death with a meat grinder. He then put her body in a closet "to get rid of her" and nailed the door shut.

The next day, one of Gibson's neighbors drove Fischer to the bus station so he could leave town. It was a month before Betty Jo Gibson's body was discovered, after some neighborhood kids noticed swarms of flies around her house.

"He gave us more (details) than the average person would have known," investigator Gene Martinez said. "Some of the cases we asked him about were publicized, but some were not."

The more Fischer talked, the higher the body count continued to grow, until it appeared he had killed 40 people, perhaps even more. But for all the horrible crimes he committed, there was one he suddenly denied—that of killing his own wife, Claudine.

"I have no memory of killing her. I loved her very much. I'd rather be dead myself. I never really had a real friend. She wasn't just a wife; she was a buddy, a friend, a pal. That's why I just can't believe what happened to her.

"I should be put in the electric chair if I did it."

In fact, Fischer wanted to be put to death. He wanted to be extradited to Oklahoma so he could receive the death penalty and be spared more years of prison. However, the one and only murder charge for which he would be prosecuted was that of his wife, Claudine Eggers, and the trial that would take place in Dutchess County would be anything but a cut and dried affair.

Trial

Almost 50 prospective jurors were dismissed during the selection process as so many had been influenced by the heavy press coverage of the alleged mass murderer. Defense attorney Denis McClure didn't help matters, as throughout the proceedings he waved stacks of newspaper articles emphasizing the many headlines in "bold banner print" that highlighted all of Fischer's confessed killings, and then grilling the individuals to see if they were aware of his client's claims.

"You mean after reading twenty articles, you didn't come to the conclusion this was a mass murderer?" he asked one prospective juror, not really helping his own case with such questions in open court.

To illustrate the results of this dubious tactic, another man who had come in with an open mind and little knowledge of Fischer said that he learned so much about the other murders from McClure harping about them, that as a result, he didn't think he could be impartial anymore.

Nonetheless, after two days a jury of five women and seven men was seated, and the trial began on April 1, 1980 with Judge Albert Rosenblatt presiding. Four New York City detectives testified that first day, describing how Fischer came into the 24th Precinct and confessed to numerous murders, including that of his wife.

"She was a bitch," Fischer had told them. "She was always bitching...I stabbed the shit out of her."

Indeed, some of the 35 stab wounds pierced Claudine Eggers' heart and lungs, and the elderly woman never had a chance. Fischer then pulled a bloody diamond ring off her finger and fled the scene.

One of the officers said he advised Fischer of his rights, but Fischer waived those rights and then said, "I want to talk to you. I like killing people."

The defense strategy was to try to get Fischer's confessions suppressed because he was drunk at the time, asserting that, "Without the confession, they (the prosecution) have no case." They also tried to establish an insanity defense, producing expert witnesses to say that Fischer suffered from pathological intoxication, and therefore was not aware of what he was doing. While the defense never admitted that their client killed his wife, if he did do it, he wasn't responsible.

"So it's a tragedy that this woman was killed, but there sits another tragedy," McClure would tell the jury. "Alcohol is a cancer of the brain…Its tentacles consume a person's understanding…The decision-making process flows from the bottle. Alcohol results in pathological intoxication, which results in the Joseph Fischers."

Assistant District Attorney Ed Gabel countered that the excuse of pathological intoxication was a "light-switch insanity" defense.

"It goes on and off when it's convenient," Gable said, as he switched the lights on and off in the courtroom. McClure immediately objected to Gabel's "ridiculous histrionics."

For three weeks the contentious court battle went on with defense and prosecution experts at odds, but all the while Fischer's own words remained as the 800-pound gorilla in the courtroom. By the time the case went to the jury, there must have been a jumble of thoughts in their minds. Did Joseph Fischer know exactly what he was doing and was therefore guilty of murder? Was he so drunk he could not be held responsible? Was he drunk, but still responsible for his actions? Did he suffer from pathological intoxication, and was that a valid condition that should exonerate him? Or, was he just simply insane?

Deliberations began around 3:30pm on April 22, but after six hours, the jury quit for the night. They returned the next morning to begin again, but it wasn't until 3:45pm that they came to a decision. Was it a good sign for the defense that it took almost 11 hours of deliberations?

According to reporters, Joseph Fischer was smiling as he sat in the courtroom awaiting the verdict. He said he was expecting to be found innocent. The suspense was finally resolved when the verdict was read, "Guilty of murder as charged."

Though vowing to appeal, Fischer told reporters what he thought of the decision, "I think it was fair. They considered everything and that's their opinion."

Perhaps he was somewhat relieved that the jury hadn't found him insane, as he also stated, "I don't want to go to the bughouse. I'd rather go to prison than to the state mental hospital."

In that regard, Fischer would get his wish.

Sentencing and Punishment

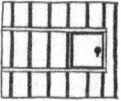

On May 16, 1980, Judge Rosenblatt sentenced Joseph Fischer to 25 years to life for the murder of his wife, Claudine Eggers. Eleven years later, in 1991, Fischer's alleged body count had risen to almost 150, but no one really bothered to try to verify all of his claims. He died that year, at age 68, and has mostly been forgotten, despite possibly being one of the country's worst mass murderers.

As to why he turned himself in that day in July of 1979, Fischer said he was "tired of running." When asked why he confessed to all of his crimes, he said it was to "cleanse his conscience."

"I feel much better. When I die and go to Claudine, I'll go to her clean. She'll accept me when the truth is out."

He added, with tears in his eyes, that he "sometimes feels" his wife is watching over him.

We will never know if Claudine Eggers continued to think that her beloved husband could do no wrong as he was stabbing her to death, or if she forgave him in the other world and was awaiting Joseph Fischer with open arms. All that is certain is that a vicious mass murderer never should have been free to go on his cross-country killing spree. How many times does a violent criminal have to victimize an innocent person before society says, "Enough!"

The High Cost of Justice

A May 16, 1980 article in the *Poughkeepsie Journal* discussed the financial costs Dutchess County incurred in the three-week murder trial of Joseph Fischer, which included 32 witnesses. The entire district attorney's office budget for all court cases for the year was $15,000, but the Fischer trial alone was estimated to cost a total of $17,000, "once all the bills were in." Such unexpected expenses cause great strain on a county's finances.

Why was the Fischer trial so expensive?

- Fischer did not have the money for a private attorney, so the county had to pay for both the prosecution and defense. A public defender at that time made about $25 an hour for in-court time, and $15 for out of court time.
- Fischer was not happy with his public defender and actually filed a civil suit claiming he was not being adequately represented, so the county had to hire two private attorneys—both of whom made far more than $25 an hour. Richard Schisler estimated his total bill to the county would be about $5,000. Denis McClure's expenses were going to be even higher than that.
- The private attorneys hired private investigators at considerable expense.
- Also, the private attorneys hired psychiatrists, such as Dr. Herman Snow, at a rate of about $75 an hour.
- The district attorney's total expenses were $7,264.

A single murder devastates so many lives, it's hard to think of something as mundane as the money involved in investigating and prosecuting these cases. However, in light of numbers such as these in the Fischer case, it's clear that there is another destructive side to serious crimes. To compensate for all of the extra money spent on lawyers, doctors, and other trial expenses, counties have to cut budgets for other programs and services. Ultimately, excessive costs will be passed on to the taxpayer.

There is an old saying that crime doesn't pay, but it certainly costs a lot, and we all end up paying the bill.

Diet Doctor's Death

Crime Scene

A buzzer went off in the caretakers' room shortly before 11pm on the stormy night of March 10, 1980. Normally, this was no cause for alarm for Mr. and Mrs. Henri Van Der Vreken; it was a simple summons by their employer, Dr. Herman Tarnower, in his luxurious, ultramodern home in Purchase, New York. However, this was different—very different—as just moments before the shocked couple had heard gunshots.

Henri raced to Tarnower's bedroom, only to find the prominent cardiologist, and famous author of the wildly popular book, *The Complete Scarsdale Medical Diet,* on the floor in his pajamas, bleeding from multiple gunshot wounds. Though seriously injured, Tarnower was still alive and Henri called the police at 10:59pm.

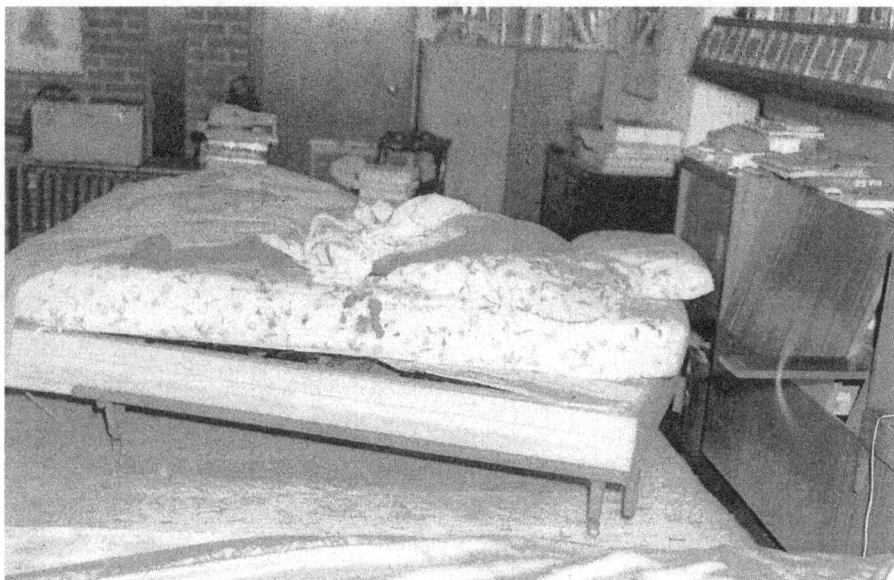

The bed is disheveled and moved out of place in Dr. Tarnower's bedroom. There are bloodstains on the mattress.   Photo courtesy of WCDA

There were signs of a struggle, and with Tarnower's reputation as a ladies' man, it wasn't a stretch to assume some jilted lover had gotten revenge on the doctor. Without an eyewitness, however, such an

90

investigation could take months, if not years, to solve. However, before Tarnower stopped breathing an hour later at St. Agnes Hospital, the potentially large pool of suspects already stood at just one.

Hair curlers, a ring, and other objects litter the floor indicating a struggle.

Photo courtesy of WCDA

Investigation

As police arrived at the scene, a car pulled up and a woman got out. She informed an officer that Dr. Tarnower had been shot. When the cop asked who did it, the woman replied, "I did."

That woman was Mrs. Jean Struven Harris, the 57-year-old, divorced headmistress at an exclusive girls' school in McLean, Virginia. How this educated, proper-appearing woman ended up in Dr. Tarnower's bedroom with a .32 caliber revolver was a story that would be splashed on newspapers' front pages across the country, along with every salacious detail that was uncovered.

Part of the tragedy, which was not generally known at the time, is that this case may have only been one of assault with a deadly weapon, had first responders acted faster in getting Tarnower to the hospital. It reportedly took half an hour just to get him out of the house. Physicians at the hospital, where Tarnower was pronounced dead at 11:58pm, said that if he had arrived just several minutes earlier they could have saved his life. As it was, internal bleeding proved fatal for the 69-year-old doctor, and Jean Harris was arrested for murder.

.32 caliber ammunition, coins, a lady's watch, and other items were found on the floor of the bathroom.   Photo courtesy of WCDA

However, Harris did not confess to murder—only to pulling the trigger. She claimed that she had driven the 264 miles in the rain from Virginia that night because she wanted to see the man she loved—and with whom she had been having an affair for 14 years—before she took her *own* life. Despondent with problems at work, she claimed she had decided to commit suicide, and at no point had any intention of hurting Tarnower. Police were immediately suspicious of this claim when they found extra ammunition in her purse and on the floor of the bathroom. After all, it only takes one bullet to commit suicide.

According to Harris' version of events, she let herself into the house and went to Tarnower's bedroom, where he had already retired for the night. She told police she just wanted to talk to him, but when she saw his young secretary's negligee and belongings in the bathroom, she became very agitated and decided to shoot herself right then and there.

When Harris placed the barrel of the revolver against her head, Tarnower tried to take the weapon away from her and the gun discharged into his hand and then went through a glass door, to which he allegedly exclaimed, "Jesus Christ, look what you've done!"

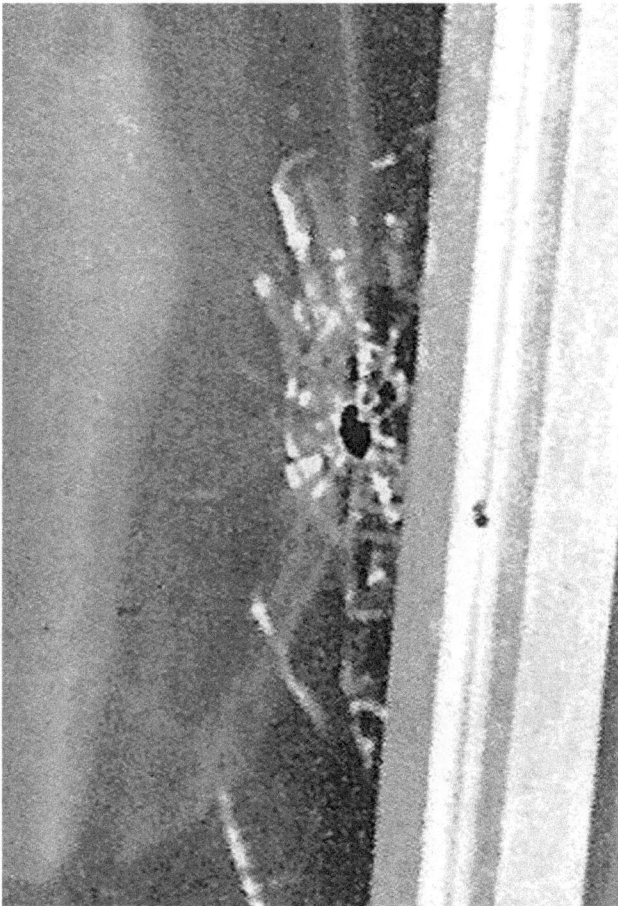

Close up of the bullet hole from the round that went through Tarnower's hand and then through a glass door. Photo courtesy of WCDA

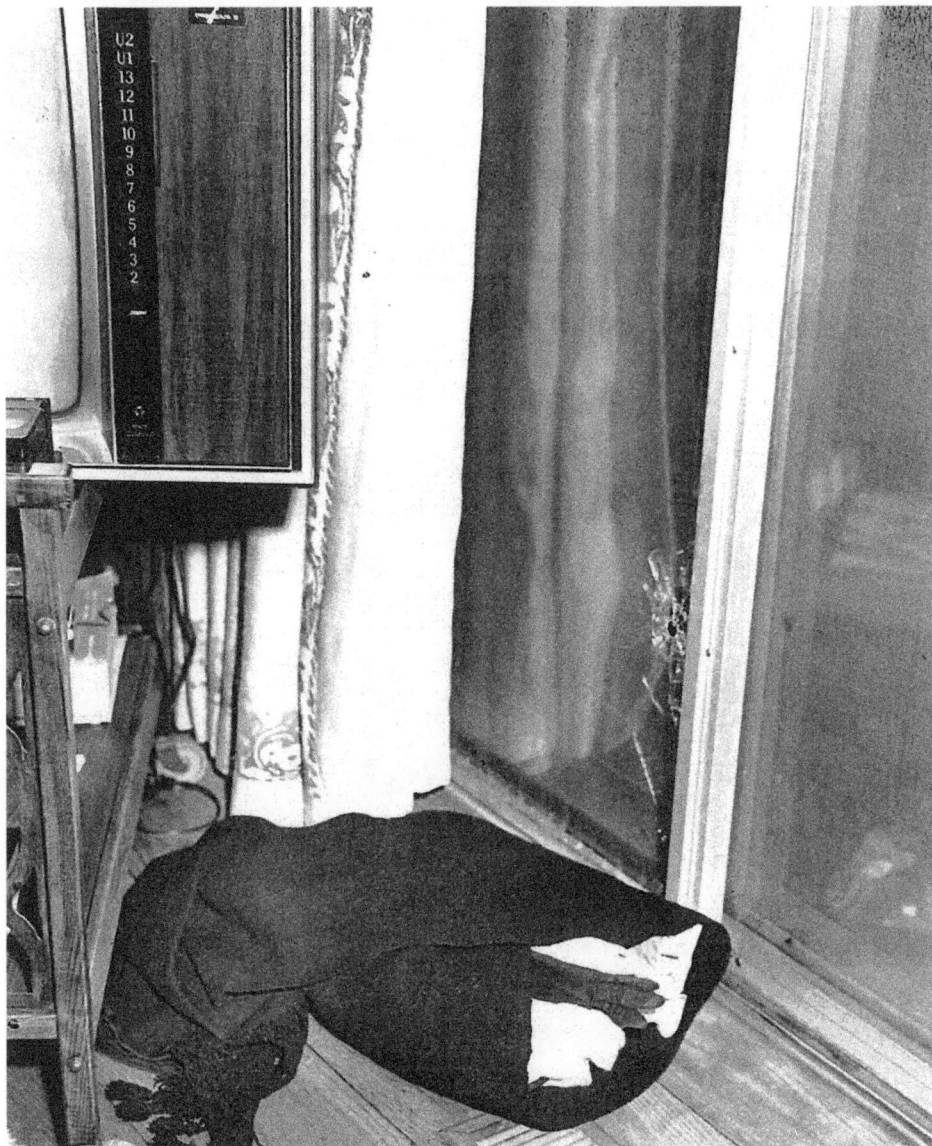

Full view of the bullet hole in the glass door.   Photo courtesy of WCDA

When Tarnower went into the bathroom to rinse the bloody wound, Harris once again tried to raise the gun to her head, and an even more intense struggle ensued. Supposedly believing that the barrel of the gun was pressed against her own body as they fought for control of the weapon, she pulled the trigger. Rather than shooting herself, though, she put three more rounds into the man she said she loved.

Harris then claimed that she pressed the .32 caliber weapon to her temple and pulled the trigger again—only there must have been an empty chamber because the gun didn't fire. Testing to see if the gun was still working, she aimed the gun *away* and put a bullet into a wooden cabinet. Why she didn't pull the trigger again when the gun was aimed at her head, if she truly desired to commit suicide, is a mystery.

The bullet hole in the back of the wooden cabinet.   Photo courtesy of WCDA

Despite sustaining four point-blank gunshot wounds, Harris stated that Tarnower didn't complain or cry out, or say so much as, "Ouch." She claimed that neither of them realized he had been shot so many times, and Harris helped him onto the bed. She then tried calling for help, but the phone wasn't working, so she decided to drive to get help. Harris said the last words they exchanged were about the phone, with her saying it wasn't working, and Tarnower simply replying, "You're probably right."

The phone on the floor by the bed, which appears to have blood on it. There are also bloodstains on the blanket and the floor. 　　　　Photo courtesy of WCDA

Harris got into her car and started to drive away, but when she saw the police driving to the house, she made a U-turn and stopped to tell them she had accidentally shot Tarnower. A bruise on her face and a swollen lip did indicate there had been a struggle, but why that struggle erupted and Harris' motives would be up to a jury to decide. The trial which was to be held in White Plains would be one of the most sensationalized courtroom dramas ever to take place in the Hudson Valley.

Trial

Harris' family raised the $80,000 to get her released until the trial, which began on November 21, 1980 at the Westchester County Courthouse. Her attorney, Joel Arnou, repeatedly urged her to plead guilty to a lesser charge, but the headstrong headmistress insisted she was not guilty of murder and wouldn't even consider any type of plea. Harris wanted complete vindication, which was a gamble that, if it failed, could mean that she would die behind bars.

The prosecutor, Assistant District Attorney George Bolen, immediately began the case by painting Jean Harris was an aging, jilted mistress in a love triangle. The other woman, Lynne Tryforos, who worked with Tarnower in his Scarsdale Medical Center, was a young, attractive, 37-year-old blonde, and jealousy drove Harris into a murderous rage. Why else would she drive five hours in terrible thunderstorms with a gun and ten rounds of ammunition, he asked the jury.

"She enters the doctor's bedroom, the lights are out," Bolen said in his opening statement. "She observes the doctor; there is a confrontation… and the defendant, armed with a .32-caliber pistol containing five live rounds of ammunition…consciously, volitionally, voluntarily, intentionally fires five shots."

12A.   Minneapolis Tribune   Mon., Oct. 12, 1981

Author: 'Deep in her heart' Jean Harris hated Tarnower

By Eileen Putman
Associated Press

New York, N.Y.
Jean Harris deeply hated Herman Tarnower, a sadistic bully to whom she crawled like an addict for sex, love and money, according to a newly published book by a longtime social critic.

"Deep in her mind and heart she wanted to kill Dr. Tarnower," Diana Trilling writes of the former Madeira School headmistress she sees as "neither fine nor ladylike."

Trilling labels Tarnower a tyrant who had "an insatiable appetite" for power and fawning women, she said in "Mrs. Harris: the Death of the Scarsdale Diet Doctor."

The book may shock Harris's de-

Herman Tarnower   Jean Harris

Newspapers across the country splashed headlines about the Diet Doctor's murder, most of which painted Harris as the jealous lover. The clippings above and below are from Arizona, Florida, Wisconsin, and Minnesota.

Harris' attorney countered by claiming in essence that this case really didn't have anything to do with Tarnower in terms of motives, that it was simply a "tragic accident" brought about by other factors. His client was despondent and suicidal over her position as headmistress of the school, not jealous or angry over her relationship with Tarnower.

"In this case the answers to the things in Jean Harris' life were in Virginia, not in New York," Aurnou, said. "How she felt about herself, her fears about aging, her depression about work, the end of her role as an active mother…a physical fatigue that was overwhelming…a state of depression well known among others and by Dr. Tarnower that finally led Jean Harris to decide abruptly, but consistent with her depression, to take her own life."

Save the wronged woman routine; doctor's killing was premeditated

Author's murder boosts book sales

So the battle lines were firmly drawn—no one questioned the fact that Harris pulled the trigger, but was it an accident, or intentional? Was there enough evidence to show that Harris had murder in her heart, or would the jury take pity on her as a sympathetic figure and believe she had only meant to harm herself? In retrospect, experts suggest that Jean Harris had a good chance of walking free had it not been for the testimony of a single witness during the unusually long, 14-week trial. That witness was Jean Harris.

Harris' own son and a friend described her as being "angry," "defensive," and "arrogant" on the stand. Rather than being a sympathetic figure, Harris' own demeanor presented a defendant that was cold, aloof, and condescending, and with a temper that was quick to flare up. Even while testifying on her own behalf in a murder trial, Harris acted the role of headmistress who expected the jury to listen to what she was saying, as if they were her students. To put it mildly, her son said his mother was "a tough cookie"—not the image one wants to portray when seeking compassion and understanding from a panel of jurors.

After one of the longest trials in New York history at that point, it took eight days of deliberation to arrive at a verdict. Because of Harris' own choices regarding the charges, the jury could not consider the lesser charge of manslaughter. They would have to decide if she was innocent or guilty of second-degree murder.

On February 24, 1981, the foreman of the jury, consisting of eight women and four men, announced the verdict—guilty. Surprisingly, however, the presiding judge, Russell Leggett, was far more sympathetic than the members of the jury had been, and later openly admitted that he didn't think Jean Harris belonged in jail, but he had no choice but to follow the law. Reluctantly, he sentenced her to 15 years to life, in a statement charged with "much emotion."

Diet doctor's jilted lover convicted

WHITE PLAINS, N.Y. (AP) — Former girls school headmistress Jean Harris was convicted Tuesday of second-degree murder in the fatal shooting of Scarsdale Diet author Dr. Herman Tarnower, her lover of 14 years who had jilted her for a younger woman.

Mrs. Harris, 57, who had been free during the three-month trial, was sent to the Westchester County jail after the jury delivered its verdict after eight days of deliberation.

The second-degree muder convic- tion, which carries a mandatory mini- mum sentence of 15 years to life, in

Mrs. Harris, former headmistress at the fashionable Madeira School for girls in McLean, Va., remanded to the jail to await sentencing on March 20.

Defense attorney Joel Aurnou said Mrs. Harris was "shocked" by the ver- dict, the harshest possible in the case.

Second-degree murder is the high- est form of murder that she could be convicted of in New York state. First- degree murder applies only to the kill- ing of law officers and prison guards, but the maximum penalty is the same.

Leggett had told the jurors that they needed only to find that, in the in- stant Mrs. Harris fired any one of the

jury, the key issues were:

✔ What was really on Mrs. Harris' mind — murder or suicide — when she drove north from her school in McLean, Va., with a loaded .32-caliber revolver last March 10?

✔ When she confronted Tarnower, 69, that night in the bedroom of his lav- ish estate in suburban Purchase, north of New York City, who really caused the gun to go off five times?

Aurnou said Mrs. Harris went there in desolation to say goodbye, kill her- self and be found lying dead and at peace beside Tarnower's duck pond.

Prosecutor George Bolen said she

Jean Harris

"Mrs. Harris, it becomes my obligation now to impose a sentence on you, and imposing a sentence is never an easy job for any judge, and it's particularly difficult for me in this case, and very particularly when I am involved with a woman who is charged with a crime, and the sentence I impose is mandated by law."

At this point the judge's voice broke and he paused before continuing.

"I wish personally, as you do, that the events of March 10 had never taken place and that you never left Virginia...I now remand you to the care and custody of the Department of Corrections, to be confined at the Bedford Hills Correctional Facility forthwith. Before I do that, Mrs. Harris, I want to advise you of your right to appeal..."

"Mrs. Harris...I found you to be a brilliant, brilliant woman...It's unhappy that you have to be sentenced, Mrs. Harris, and the best I can say to you is, the best of luck to you."

If only the verdict had also been left up to the judge, it appears as if Jean Harris would have been a free woman! But as it stood, she was promptly handcuffed and brought to Bedford Hills, possibly for 15 years, and possibly for the rest of her life.

Punishment and Aftermath

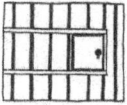

The courts determined that Harris had received a fair trial, so her appeals were all denied. By all accounts she became an exemplary inmate, helping fellow prisoners earn their GEDs and working tirelessly on parenting programs for women who gave birth in prison. But Harris, the convicted murderer, yet ever the headmistress, also complained about the deplorable language in prison and thought the corrections officers should also "correct" all of the swearing that went on!

In the long history of homicide, it isn't often we get to hear the in-depth stories of the events and motives from the perpetrators themselves, but as this had been such a sensationalized case, it attracted widespread attention of the media in general, and the famous journalist Barbara Walters, in particular. Walters arranged for not one, but two interviews with Jean Harris, which at the time was "must see TV," and is still fascinating to watch even after all these years.

Looking very much as if she was dressed for an outing at a country club with some friends, rather than being in prison, Harris spoke of her great love for the man she called "Hy" and explained that theirs had been an open relationship from the start. She was well aware of all of his other women—as he never attempted to conceal them—and had known for many years that she was sharing Tarnower with Lynne Tryforos, so the idea that she had suddenly gone into a jealous rage was nonsense.

Then Harris bristled when Walters said the media had portrayed her as an aging mistress.

"I'm aging, but *not* a mistress. Now or ever!"

She further explained:

"I was devoted to Hy. There was one person in the world I wanted to see before I died and that was Hy. The happiest moments of my life I spent with Hy, the most interesting, the most stimulating, the most depressing, the most all different kinds. Hy was a very different man, and very selfish, as I think the most interesting people are apt to be. He was more interesting to me than any other man I ever met."

In the first interview, Harris steadfastly maintained that she had done the right thing by testifying; she denied appearing to be cold on the stand, and said she wouldn't have been able to live with herself if she hadn't told her side of the story, in her own way. However, during the second interview, Harris finally conceded that her testimony probably didn't help her case.

What also didn't help her was the fact that the jury was not aware that, at the time of the murder, Harris was addicted to powerful amphetamines that Tarnower had been prescribing her for years. Even she wasn't aware of her addiction until she went to prison, as she continued to be given the drug throughout her trial. Because of fatigue from her stressful job, Harris had been taking Desoxyn, which is the highly-addictive methamphetamine hydrochloride, known to cause sleeplessness, restlessness, and even hallucinations. Today, doctors and countless websites warn that no one should take Desoxyn who is prone to "severe anxiety, tension, or agitation."

Jean Harris was a ticking time bomb of stress, depression, and methamphetamine when she went to Tarnower's home the night of March 10, 1980. Of course, none of this excuses what she did. She could have chosen to seek professional help with her problems. At any point in the 264-mile drive up the east coast in bad weather, she could have chosen to stop and turn around. If she had only wanted to see Tarnower before she killed herself, she did not have to bring a loaded gun into his bedroom. Yet to a jury, amphetamine addiction, for which Tarnower had written the years and years of prescriptions, might have tempered their opinions as to the clarity and state of Harris' mind.

Barbara Walters grew quite close to Harris during their interviews, to the point where her bosses told her to stop, as she was no longer able to be objective. Walters also personally called the governor of New York, many times, asking him to grant Harris clemency. It appeared that, like the judge at her trial, Harris had managed to gain another ally.

Harris' son also tirelessly worked to get his mother out of prison, where she suffered three heart attacks over the years. After serving over

11 years, and facing quadruple bypass surgery, on December 29, 1992, New York Governor Mario Cuomo granted Jean Harris clemency.

Once free, she had a third interview with Barbara Walters.

"Prison made me stronger," she told Walters. "You either stand for something, or you fold."

Harris insisted her years behind bars were not wasted, and she continued to stand for her causes of education and parenting after her release. She passed away on December 23, 2012 at the age of 89, and a very long, strange chapter in Hudson Valley history drew to a close.

No one can ever say for certain whether or not Jean Harris had murder in her heart the night she shot and killed Dr. Herman Tarnower. The only thing about which we can be sure is this—for a very smart lady, she made a series of fatally bad decisions.

Additional Notes

Jean Harris was at the top of the list of acknowledgements in Tarnower's highly successful diet book. Lynne Tryforos was also in the list.

Tarnower had left the sum of $220,000 in his will for Harris, but because she was convicted of his murder she was not eligible to collect it.

In the 1985 book "Coroner at Large," Dr. Thomas Noguchi and Herbert MacDonnell examined the crime scene—which had been preserved for four years!—as well as previously unseen police photos. They concluded that the evidence showed that there had been a struggle for the gun, as Harris had claimed, and therefore she was indeed innocent of the charge of second-degree murder.

Interestingly, Jean Harris had shot Tarnower in Purchase, NY, which was in the Town of Harrison, whose Chief of Police was William Harris (no relation).

Tarnower hosted a dinner party at his home the night he was shot, and his guests included his sister and Lynne Tryforos. On November 28, 1981, the *Pittsburgh Press* reported that the following conversation had taken place after dinner:

That night, as the talk bubbled in the two-level, somewhat spare but attractive and comfortable living room, furnished with fine traditional pieces and many rare objets d'art from his world travels, the conversation touched on murder for several moments. A novel, in which three women murdered their husbands, was under discussion. Tarnower, jokingly and with a wink, said that that was one of the advantages of being a bachelor, that it could never happen to him.

The Last Call Killer

Crime Scene

On Saturday, July 31, 1993, third-generation hot dog vendor Ron Colandrea thought someone had dumped household garbage in the trash cans he used at the parking location of his food truck on Route 9W in Haverstraw, New York, overlooking the Hudson River. This wouldn't be the first time, and Colandrea routinely went through the bags of garbage looking for anything that had an address on it, so he could write a letter requesting that the people stop leaving their trash in his cans. However, the first heavy plastic bag he opened did not contain household trash, but the severed head of a man! The man's arms were also in the trash, but the legs and torso were missing.

"He had to be dumped overnight," Colandrea told the *Journal News*, "It was still fresh and there were no flies."

Colandrea tore open a small hole in the white plastic bag and discovered that a severed head was inside.
All photos courtesy of the
Rockland County Sheriff's Bureau of Criminal Investigation.

Colandrea had noted that there wasn't any blood on the outside of the bag, or on the trashcan, to indicate its grisly contents. Had he not been so conscientious about the trash, this man's body parts would have ended up in the dump.

Crime scene tape cordons off the hot dog truck overlooking the Hudson River, with the trash can that contained the body parts on the right.

He noted that the head was large, so it must have been a big man, and this man had a closely-trimmed beard. Colandrea also made several other observations of the body parts.

"He had a gash on the front left side of his head. It looked like his arms were cut nice and even like butchering a cow."

One of the first cops to arrive, Haverstraw Police Officer Ed Devoe, said it was a "sickening sight." When authorities realized the rest of the body was missing, they closed a one mile stretch of Route 9W and brought in dogs to see if they could find the other pieces. When a wallet and attaché case were recovered, they were able to put a possible name on the dismembered corpse—Michael J. Sakara, 56, who lived and worked in Manhattan.

While police continued scouring the crime scene, Colandrea bemoaned the fact that he knew he would "lose customers today," because of the awful discovery in his trash cans. A *Journal News* reporter spoke to an elderly woman who had stopped to eat, but decided to leave when she heard the horrible news.

"I couldn't eat hot dogs now," she said.

On August 8, one week after the hot dog vendor discovered the severed head and arms in Haverstraw, volunteer fireman James Beninson was riding his motorcycle on Route 9W and stopped alongside the road in Stony Point, about nine miles to the north. Beninson was aware of the gruesome discovery the week before, and when he looked over the guardrail and saw four green plastic bags, he became suspicious. Upon closer inspection, he noticed a foul odor and the outline of a leg in one of the bags. Inside were the "rotting" and "maggot-infested" remains of the missing pieces of Michael Sakara.

Michael Sakara

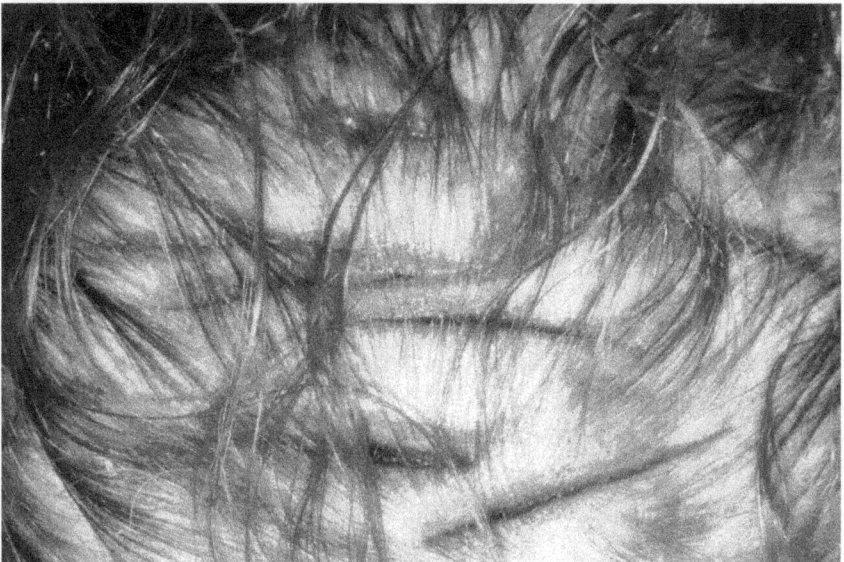

Some of the brutal head wounds found during the autopsy of Michael Sakara.

Investigation

Obviously, the killer had gone to great lengths to dismember his victim into seven pieces and deposit them in multiple locations. However, by the time the legs and torso were discovered, a positive identification had already taken place, with the victim's fingerprints confirming he had indeed been Michael Sakara, a law journal typesetter who lived in New York City. The cause of death was "severe head injuries," but he had also been stabbed several times. Tests showed that Sakara had been "under the influence" of alcohol when he was killed.

Police began tying together Sakara's life, and his movements on his last day. Reporters were also hot on the trail and spoke to the doorman where Sakara lived.

"His lover would sometimes be dressed like a woman when he walked out of the building with Mr. Sakara," the doorman said, adding that everyone knew the couple was gay.

However, Sakara and his boyfriend had split months earlier, and the other man was not suspected of the crime. Police then spoke to the employees of the 5 Oaks piano bar in Greenwich Village, where bartender Lisa Hall was very well acquainted with Sakara, a regular, whom she said was a wonderful person. Hall provided valuable information, telling police that on the night of the murder, Sakara was with a man named John or Mark, and that he was a nurse at St. Vincent's Hospital. They left the bar together at 4:30am, and that was the last time Sakara was ever seen.

Authorities then obtained information and photos of all of the male nurses at St. Vincent's, as well as those from other area hospitals. Hall thought she recognized the man with whom Sakara was seen leaving the bar that night—Richard Rogers, a nurse at Mount Sinai Medical Center, who lived in Staten Island and frequented both the 5 Oaks and Townhouse gay bars. However, as his

Richard Rogers

name wasn't John or Mark, and he didn't work at St. Vincent's, that lead was not pursued.

There weren't any other leads until cops learned that this shocking murder and dismemberment fit the profile of the murders of at least three other gay men. This was not just a single act by a deranged killer; this was a very dangerous serial killer.

The other victims were:

Peter Anderson: A divorced investment broker with two children, who lived in Philadelphia. On May 5, 1991, six green plastic bags containing his dismembered body parts were discovered along the Pennsylvania Turnpike. On May 6, Dr. Isidore Mihalakis at the Lancaster County Morgue reported that in addition to multiple stab wounds, Anderson's penis had been cut off and "stuffed inside the mouth and pushed far into the throat." Retracing the steps of the last day Anderson was seen, which was May 3, authorities determined that he had spent the evening at the Townhouse bar on East 58th Street in Manhattan, and was reportedly very intoxicated when he left.

Peter Anderson

Thomas Mulcahy: A 55-year-old salesman from Massachusetts who was married and had four children. On July 10, 1992, the pieces of his body were discovered in seven white and brown plastic trash bags at two roadside stops in Ocean and Burlington Counties in New Jersey. Mulcahy had been at the World Trade Center in Manhattan to give a presentation on July 8, and was last seen that night in the Townhouse bar. He had been stabbed to death, and was also quite intoxicated when he died.

Thomas Mulcahy   Anthony Marrero

Anthony Marrero: A 44-year-old male prostitute who worked near the Port Authority Bus Terminal in Manhattan. On May 10, 1993, at 7:30 a.m., a motorist in New Jersey came upon a severed arm with rope tied to it. When police arrived at the scene, they found six green plastic bags containing more dismembered parts of a man. Inside one of those green bags, the man's head was in a shopping bag printed with the words "Thank You," which authorities traced to several Acme stores, one of which was on Staten Island. Cause of death was seven stab wounds, six of which were in the back. Toxicology reports were positive for marijuana.

In the Marrero case, two fingerprints and a palm print were recovered from two of the plastic bags, but there were no hits on AFIS (Automated Fingerprint Identification System). With the obvious connection to the gay community in Manhattan, interviews were conducted, but no one seemed willing to talk to police. Despite a joint task force that consisted of the Rockland County District Attorney's Office, the New York City Police, the Ocean County Prosecutor's Office, the New Jersey State Police, and the Pennsylvania State Police, the case quickly went cold. The task force was disbanded and for the next six years it appeared as if this serial killer had gotten away with at least four horrific murders. And either the serial killer stopped killing—which would be highly unusual—or he changed his modus operandi, as no more plastic bags of dismembered body parts were found.

However, Mulcahy's wife, Margaret, did not give up, and in 1999 she hired a private investigator and contacted the New Jersey State Police to see if there were any new leads. As forensic technology had improved over those years, another task force was formed in 2000 to reexamine the evidence. One of the new advancements was Vacuum Metal Deposition, a method developed by Canadian police to find fingerprints which could not be detected by conventional means.

The plastic bags in the Mulcahy case were sent to the Toronto Police who were able to find sixteen prints that matched those found in the Marrero case. Now certain that the same man had committed both murders, the prints were sent to every state database. On May 14, 2001, the Rockland County District Attorney's Office received a call that a match had been found. A fingerprint analyst from Maine finally put a name to this monster: Richard Westall Rogers, Jr., the nurse at Mount Sinai who lived in Staten Island, whom Lisa Hall had identified in 1993.

For further confirmation, Pennsylvania State Police were later able to identify eighteen fingerprints and one palm print from Richard Rogers that were found in the evidence of the Peter Anderson murder.

As they were dealing with someone capable of such inhuman acts of violence and barbarity, the police decided to approach Rogers at Mount Sinai Hospital under the pretense that someone had been making fraudulent charges on Rogers' credit card. Thinking that he was the victim of a crime, Rogers willingly accompanied the officers to police headquarters on May 27, 2001.

Rogers reportedly maintained his calm demeanor even after Lieutenant Thomas Hayes of the Ocean County Prosecutor's Office and Detective David Dalrymple of the New Jersey State Police began questioning him about the murders of the four men. He even quickly identified Sakara from the photos he was shown, explaining that they had both frequented the 5 Oaks bar, but then calmly stated that there wasn't anything else he could help the police with in these cases. Hayes later remarked that Rogers was "very polite at the time, very cooperative."

Switching the subject, Hayes and Dalrymple wanted to find out more about Rogers, and he volunteered the information that he liked to travel, and had been all across the country. This is not something law enforcement wants to hear about a vicious serial killer, as that greatly expands his "killing fields." In fact, Rogers was later linked to the 1982 murder of 21-year-old Matthew Jon Pierro in Florida. Pierro had been strangled and stabbed, and one of his nipples had been bitten off. Rogers' dental impression matched the bite wound.

Six years later, in August of 1988, Rogers was arrested in New York City when 47-year-old Frederick Lerro accused him of assault and unlawful imprisonment. Lerro claimed that he had met Rogers at a gay bar. He asserts that he was drugged by Rogers, and when he regained consciousness, he was tied up and Rogers was beating him. The man somehow managed to get away alive, unlike Rogers' other victims. However, a judge in a nonjury trial acquitted Rogers of all charges in December of 1988, and the polite, smiling, kind, convincing serial killer was set free to continue his reign of terror and violence.

"Richard was the kind of neighbor that everyone wished to have," one of his neighbors said about him.

While he may have been a great neighbor, he wasn't such a good roommate, and authorities missed a golden opportunity to get this monster off the streets way back in 1973. As a 22-year-old graduate student at the University of Maine, Rogers was arrested when Frederick Spencer's body was found by two bicyclists along a desolate section of road. Spencer was shirtless, his skull had been crushed, and his body had been wrapped in a tent and dumped.

Rogers explained that it was all Spencer's fault. Rogers was the victim, as Spencer came at him with a hammer. Rogers was only defending himself when he took the hammer away from his roommate and pounded on Spencer's head with eight deadly blows. At least, that was his side of the story. As a lawyer involved in the trial later said, it was Roger's word against that of a dead man.

The blossoming serial killer somehow managed to impress upon the jury that he was completely innocent—even though he then attempted to conceal the bloody deed and dumped Spencer's body, rather than call

111

police. Rogers was acquitted of the murder, and this case is a testament his amazing ability to lie and conceal his brutal homicidal nature beneath a benign and charming exterior.

In Norwich Man's Death

Murder Charge Dismissed in Me.

Headline from the Binghamton, NY *Press and Sun Bulletin* on November 3, 1973.

However, even with the irrefutable evidence against him in the Anderson, Mulcahy, Marerro, and Sakara slayings, Rogers bent, but did not break during his interrogation. When Hayes finally revealed that Rogers had been brought in to be charged for these crimes, his demeanor changed from being open and friendly, to very nervous, and according to the investigators, he suddenly became quite flatulent. As Hayes delineated all of the fingerprint evidence, Rogers apparently was silent and only nodded his head. He neither confessed nor denied the accusations.

Remarkably, being faced with murder charges, he then asked, "Do you think I need a lawyer? Should I consult with an attorney?" And with that, the initial interview was over, but Rogers was finally behind bars.

When cops searched Rogers' home, they did not find any body parts or weapons, but they did find Versed, a potential date rape drug, as it calms a person and puts them to sleep. Upon waking, the person will have no memory of recent events. Even more disturbing discoveries were the "several photographs of unknown men on which stab wounds had been drawn." For example, Rogers had taken a photo of a shirtless construction worker and then drawn a red line down his torso as if he had been cut.

Then there was a Bible which had marked passages speaking about killing, and the chopping off of heads and hands. Whether or not Rogers somehow found justification for his crimes from these passages, he never said. Rogers also never revealed where the murders actually occurred, or where he cut up and cleaned the bodies.

Fortunately, authorities didn't need Rogers' confession. They had the fingerprint evidence. It was now time to see if Rogers—who the press dubbed "The Last Call Killer" for his pattern of picking up men at bars at closing time—could once again charm his way past a judge and jury.

Trial

Richard Rogers would go on trial for the murders of Thomas Mulcahy and Anthony Marerro in Ocean County, New Jersey in the fall of 2005. After several hearings, the presiding judge allowed evidence from the Anderson and Sakara murders to also be introduced by the prosecution, because of the remarkable similarity in the manner of death, dismemberment, and disposal of the bodies.

While Rogers maintained he was innocent, he did not take the stand this time, so he did not have the opportunity to weave a convincing web of lies. The trial lasted three and a half weeks, as the prosecution put forth a devastating litany of damning evidence in gory, gruesome detail. On November 10, 2005, Richard Westall Rogers, Jr. was found guilty.

Sentencing and Punishment

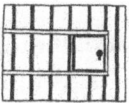

On January 27th, 2006, Rogers was sentenced to serve two consecutive sentences of 30 years to life. He is currently in the New Jersey State Prison in Trenton, and is not eligible for parole until 2066.

Both the Rockland County District Attorney and Pennsylvania authorities decided not to prosecute Rogers in separate trials for the murders of Sakara and Anderson, but in the end, more convictions wouldn't have changed anything. Richard Rogers will never get out of prison alive. His victims will not be brought back to life. The trail of terror and violence that traumatized so many people cannot be undone.

We are only left to wonder how many green plastic bags that were dumped into trash cans were never discovered, and in how many states across the country over how many decades did Richard Rogers smile, and charm, and stab, and dismember?

113

Stone Cold Furnace Murderer

Crime Scene

In 1934, the Pel-Hutchinson apartment building at 590 East 3rd Street in Mount Vernon, NY was one of the most exclusive residences in town. At around 5pm on Sunday, October 14, an employee of the apartment complex, Carl Hutchinson, wanted to adjust the oil furnace, so he went outside and around to the basement door on the Warwick Avenue side of the building, and was puzzled when he found the door locked. Heading back inside, he took the elevator down and then began descending a staircase to the lowest level, where the furnace room was located.

Along the way, Hutchinson noticed what appeared to be drops of blood on the stairs and in the hallways. Then in the furnace room, there was an unmistakable pool of blood right in front of the blazing furnace. Fearing that something terrible had happened, he quickly ran to call the police, and didn't even stop when he thought he saw a dark figure lurking in the basement.

Detective Frank Springer responded, and Hutchinson showed him to the furnace. Slowly opening the furnace door, both men were horrified to find the charred bones of a small child.

Investigation

Detective Springer reported the gruesome find, and another police vehicle carrying two more detectives and a patrolman were dispatched. Just a short distance from the apartment building, there was an accident with another vehicle and the policemen were injured. An ambulance arrived at the scene and the policemen got inside. A young man with blood on his shirt and pants got inside the ambulance as well, claiming that he was also injured. Once at the hospital, doctors examined the young man and couldn't find any wounds. So where had all that blood come from?

As a child had been murdered and there was blood at the scene of the crime, and this man, covered in blood, had been near the apartment building, he was brought to police headquarters for questioning. As the hours after the discovery of the burnt remains ticked by, investigators heard from multiple eyewitnesses that a man, Lawrence Clinton Stone, had been seen in front of the apartment building playing ball with 5-year-old Nancy Jean Costigan of Forrest Hills, NY. Nancy had been staying there with her aunt, Mrs. Russell Newhouse, for the week. Stone had been previously employed at the Pel-Hutchinson apartments so residents had recognized him.

After ten hours of intense interrogation by District Attorney Frank Coyne, Chief Inspector Michael Silverstein, and Detective James Gleason, 24-year-old Lawrence Stone confessed to the unthinkable:

We were playing ball in the cellar. I threw the ball and hit her on the head. She toppled over and fell on the cellar floor, smacking her head. Her face turned blue and I didn't know what to do. She started bleeding from the mouth.

I picked her up and ran around the cellar with her, not knowing what to do. I first was going to bring her upstairs, but I got frightened. It then came to my head to take her to the boiler room and I disposed of her by placing her body in the furnace, the fire not burning.

I then ran out, not knowing what to do. I walked up East 3rd Street to Columbus Avenue, when I seen an automobile accident. I seen an automobile coming out of Columbus Avenue, from the direction of 4th Street, which struck a police automobile. I ran over to help out the occupants who I recognized as Louis Scarpino and John Gleason, two police officers.

The blood which was on both of my hands and necktie which is now in the possession of the police came from the child while I was carrying her in my arms to the boiler room. I alone am responsible for her death and no one else.

I am awfully sorry for the trouble I made for the child's parents who were always friendly to me. I am making this statement of my own free will and accord so I may get it off my mind.

Lawrence Clinton Stone

Newspapers had a field day with the "Furnace Murderer" who had coldly and cruelly "cremated a little girl," and the story and his picture were in headlines across the country. The sensational murder story even made it as far as Australia. Everyone wanted to know who was this monster, and how could he have done such a thing?

115

Fire Slayer, Victim and Death Furnace

Associated Press Photo.

Upper left, Nancy Jean Costigan, 5, of Forest Hills, L. I., whose burned body was found in an apartment house furnace in Mount Vernon. Upper right, Clarence Stone, hatless, center, a discharged handyman, being led away by police officials for questioning. They say he confessed. Lower right, Medical Examiner Amos O. Squire and a police officer examining the firebox of the furnace after the body had been removed.

Works as Usual On 91st Birthday

John C. Mullins is 91 today and his reaction at reaching this milestone can be summed up in two words—"So what?"

Newspapers like the *Brooklyn Daily Eagle* splashed headlines about the murder and posed law enforcement officials at the furnace and with other evidence in the case.

Youth Admits He Stuffed Girl Alive Into Furnace

By NEIL PATTERSON.

Lawrence Stone, 24-year-old hallboy, admitted to Mount Vernon police late yesterday that he knew Nancy Jean Costigan, 5, was alive when he stuffed her body into a furnace, District Attorney Frank H. Coyne of Westchester County stated last night.

Lawrence Stone

"I knew she was alive when I put her in there, but I didn't know the flames were on," the prisoner declared, according to a statement Coyne made after communicating with Mount Vernon authorities.

A vista of swift death in the electric chair opened before Stone as the police sought to augment his confession to slaying and cremating the child, with a further admission that he attacked and tortured her before thrusting her into the fire.

Hamilton Anderson, Manhattan attorney, who spends Summers at New Milford, Conn., Stone's birth-

Detective Tom Tierney with pocketbook and ball belonging to little Jean. "We were playing ball together," Stone told police.

place, visited the prisoner late yes-

The late Nancy Jean Costigan
(NEWS photo)

basement because of fears of an attempt to lynch the prisoner.

That Stone had mistreated the child in the basement of the smart Pel-Hutchinson Apartments at 590 E. 3d St., Mount Vernon, was a foregone conclusion in the mind of Chief Inspector Michael I. Silverstein of Mount Vernon who listened to Stone's sobbing confession at 3:45 A. M. yesterday.

Already Branded as Slayer.

Already Dr. Amos O. Squire, County Medical Examiner, had charged the jobless and powerful poolroom loafer with first degree murder. Until Stone recants his statement that he killed the child by accident, however, presentation

The *Daily News* was not alone in using shocking headlines, October 16, 1934

One article stated:

"Stone, according to records at the Connecticut State reformatory, where he was confined for two years, was 'definitely feeble-minded.' He also served a term in a detention home and a short period in state prison for robbery. His family was once wealthy, he said yesterday. He did not even know now where his mother was."

Indeed, the Stone family could trace its roots back to the Mayflower, and at one point they "owned half of Litchfield County" in Connecticut. However, Lawrence Stone had alienated most of his family, but he was still in contact with one brother, who owned a mechanic shop in Mount Vernon. In fact, "the jobless and powerful poolroom loafer," as one newspaper called Lawrence, had slept in one of the cars at his brother's shop the night before.

It was later learned that Stone's mother, Mrs. Otis Horton, was living in Staatsburg, NY with her third husband. One of his half-brothers, Leroy Roezell, was in county jail awaiting trial for assault and robbery, and another brother, Raymond, worked at the Hudson River State Hospital. Lawrence Stone's trouble with the law began in 1923 when he was first sentenced for theft, at the age of just 12, and he spent two years in the Connecticut School for Boys in Meriden. In 1927, "he ran afoul of the law on a similar charge" and was sent to the state reformatory.

Reporters swarmed the neighborhood looking for any new angle, and found this interesting story about Stone's hours before the murder:

Stone spent the afternoon in an East 3rd Street café reading a book and drinking beer. When he left he forgot to take the book, a copy of "Missing Men," by Captain John Ayres, formerly of the New York Police Department.

Stone had inserted a marker at a chapter headed "Murder" and dealing with the Becker-Rosenthal case.[1]

---

[1] In 1915, NYPD Lt. Charles Becker was executed in the electric chair in Sing Sing prison for his part in the 1912 murder of Herman Rosenthal, who ran an illegal gambling establishment. Rosenthal was about to testify against Becker, whom he claimed was a crooked cop who not only held the mortgage on the gambling building, but had been collecting 20% of the profits. Four other people were also executed for the crime, and there was a political domino effect as a result of the widespread corruption.

"Crime doesn't pay," was a sentence on the marked page.

"And I know myself," said Stone, when it was called to his attention, "that crime don't pay."

On October 16, the *Daily News* fanned the flames of outrage by reporting:

A vista of swift death in the electric chair opened before Stone as the police sought to augment his confession to slaying and cremating the child, with a further admission that he attacked and tortured her before thrusting her into the fire.

New Confession Speeds Furnace Slayer to Chair

Armed with a new confession from Lawrence Stone, 24, Westchester authorities will ask the Grand Jury today for a first-degree murder indictment to send him to the electric chair for slaying 5-year-old Nancy Jean Costigan, whose body he stuffed into a Mount Vernon apartment house furnace.

Stone's new statement, according to Assistant District Attorney Thomas D. Scoble Jr., provided what has been lacking—a reason for the crime. It caused Scoble to discard the previous theory that Nancy was murdered after being criminally assaulted.

May Have Taunted Him.

The prosecutor was mysteriously silent regarding Stone's explanation, but indicated the State will say Nancy herself gave some childish provocation which caused Stone, whose prison records declare him to be feebleminded, to strike her.

The girl's head struck the floor

Lawrence Stone

Indeed, to Silverstein "it was a forgone conclusion" that Stone had done far more to little Nancy than played ball. A blood smear was found on Stone's leg *under* his pants, which certainly suggested his pants were off or down at some point. Residents became so enraged at the possible rape and murder of an innocent child that "A crowd of nearly 1000 persons surged around Mount Vernon headquarters last night, causing heavy guards to be posted outside and necessitating the postponement of a scheduled reconstruction of the crime in the apartment house basement because of fears of an attempt to lynch the prisoner."

Then it got even worse. At one point, Stone admitted that he strangled the little girl to silence her screams, but wouldn't admit that she was screaming because he was attacking her. Stone then added to his confession by stating that knew Nancy was *still alive* when he put her in the furnace! However, he steadfastly maintained that the furnace was not on, which was just one of many lies he told police, who were able to confirm that the furnace had been burning constantly for at least 24 hours. In fact, one officer who examined the furnace that day said the "flames were leaping 6 feet high."

It seemed as if nothing would keep Stone form burning in the electric chair, but there was still the possibility of an insanity defense. After all, what sane man attacks a little girl and throws her—alive—into an inferno?

On February 6, 1935, the Mount Vernon newspaper, *The Daily Argus*, reported that a state panel had declared that Stone was sane and therefore would be going to trial—a trial to determine whether or not he would be sentenced to death. However, if people expected that the specter of life in prison would make Stone cower in fear, they were in for a surprise.

Stone declared that he was quite happy in jail:

"Among other things I got a swell haircut and I feel 100 percent better. In other words, I feel right at home and I am sitting on top of the world."

Prosecutors and the public hoped that Stone would soon be sitting in the electric chair.

Trial

 Stone's attorney, Elliott Cohen, was prepared to fight the charge of first degree murder as he maintained his client was not mentally competent, despite what the state experts had asserted. Cohen pointed to the records of the Cheshire Reformatory, where Stone's IQ was found to be 59, as well as the state's own words that Stone's "mentality was low," and he claimed that his client operated at the intellectual level of an eight or nine-year-old. He should not go to prison, Cohen maintained, but to an institution where he could be cared for instead.

In another extremely bizarre twist to this case, while awaiting trial, Stone's jail cell was near that of Albert Fish (see next chapter), arguably the most depraved child serial killer in history. The two developed a mutual hatred and contempt of one another, but both were very interested in each other's cases as they faced similar consequences. In fact, Stone was fully prepared to go to court and fight his charges, until Fish was sentenced to die in the electric chair.

Reportedly, upon hearing this news, he "collapsed" on the floor of his cell and began "moaning." Then "Stone banged his head against his cell wall until restrained by guards." Soon after, a lot of closed door meetings took place between Cohen and the District Attorney's office. Then news came that in order to avoid the electric chair, Stone was willing to plead guilty to second degree murder. His plea was accepted, as it would spare the Costigan family the horror of reliving all of the details of the case during a trial.

Sentencing and Punishment

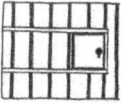

As Stone had pled guilty to the crime, all that was left was the sentencing. On March 25, 1935, Cohen gave an "impassioned plea for leniency" before New York State Supreme Court Justice William F. Bleakley. Cohen talked about how Stone had lacked any parental guidance as his father died when he was young, and his mother remarried so many times. Then after reform school in Connecticut, he was left to wander around on his own, sleeping in a tiny shack and living off charity.

Cohen went on to say that "Unfortunate circumstances forced this boy to the scene of the crime," as he was to be paid a mere 25 cents for a menial job at a road construction project in front of the building. Cohen then quickly added that Nancy's death was actually "an unfortunate accident."

Given Stone's mental challenges, his lack of a home life, and the trauma allegedly inflicted by the reform school, Cohen then concluded that, "If responsibility is to be placed for this crime, it should be placed on the State of Connecticut."

Justice Bleakley replied to Cohen's dramatic speech by stating, "We must protect our children by putting this man in a place where he will not be able to harm anybody for life." Bleakley then pronounced the sentence—50 years to life.

STONE GETS FIFTY YEARS FOR COSTIGAN MURDER

Stone's only reaction was to exclaim, "Half a century!"

It was reported that Stone also "whined" that he thought he would only get 20 years. Justice Bleakley told him he was "lucky not to go to the chair."

That very same day, Lawrence Stone was sent off to Sing Sing prison in Ossining, NY—handcuffed to Albert Fish, of all people! The newspapers then appear to have forgotten him, and only one reference could be found that Stone was eventually sent to a State Hospital, the assumption being that his sanity did come into question at some point.

We can only hope that he never again became a free man.

YOUNG AND OLD ENTER SING SING

Handcuffed to each other, 65-year-old Albert Fish, center, and Lawrence Clinton Stone, right, are pictured with a deputy entering Sing Sing prison at Ossining, N. Y., to pay the penalty for crime. Fish, convicted of slaying 10-year-old Grace Budd of New York in 1928, faces death in the electric chair. Stone, descendant of a pioneer Connecticut family, is sentenced to 50 years to life for the furnace killing of little Nancy Jean Costigan in Mount Vernon, N. Y., last October. The Costigan child was from Chicago.

Article in the *Hammond Times* of Indiana, March, 1935.

122

RECEIVING BLOTTER

NUMBER 89273 NAME Lawrence Clinton Stone   CLASSIFICATION GROUP ....

ALIAS ....

SENTENCED 3/25/35 RECEIVED 3/25/35 FROM Westchester COUNTY..........

GRADE B COLOR W COURT Supreme JUDGE Bleakley

PLEA Cont. CRIME Murder 2nd

TERM 50-0/Life LOST TIME .... JAIL TIME 161

ELIGIBLE FOR PAROLE 4/7/68

CRIMINAL ACT Killed Nancy Jean Costigan— DATE OF COMMISSION 10/14/34

CITY OR TOWN WHERE CRIME WAS COMMITTED Mt. Vernon, N.Y.

VALUE OF GOODS OR MONEY INVOLVED IN CRIME .... RECOVERED? ....

ACCOMPLICES .... WHERE ARE THEY NOW? ....

IS PRISONER ON FRIENDLY TERMS WITH ACCOMPLICES? ....

DATE OF BIRTH Dec. 27, 190 AGE 24 YEARS, MENTAL AGE .... MENTAL DIAGNOSIS ....

CITY New Milford STATE Conn. DATE OF ENTRY TO U.S. ....

NATIVITY ....

COUNTRY .... PORT OF ENTRY TO U.S. ....

CITY .... STATE .... DEAD   CITY .... STATE N.Y. DEAD
NATIVITY OF FATHER COUNTRY U.S.A.   LIVING NATIVITY OF MOTHER COUNTRY .... LIVING

AGE OF PRISONER WHEN FATHER DIED 5   WHEN MOTHER DIED ....

NUMBER OF BROTHERS 3 living SISTERS 1 living   SEQUENCE IN FAMILY 4th

SINGLE ✓ MARRIED .... WIDOWED .... DIVORCED .... SEPARATED .... COMMON LAW MARRIAGE .... HOW LONG ....

NUMBER OF CHILDREN ....   MODERATE
HABITS, TEMPERATE   DRUG Smoke Aspirin Tablets
INTEMPERATE ✓ USES   TOBACCO ....

HEIGHT .... WEIGHT ....   GOOD ✓ AGE LEFT SCHOOL 13
READ ✓
EDUCATION WRITE ✓ ENGLISH, OTHER LANGUAGE ....   HEALTH ....
SPEAKS ENGLISH PARTIAL
GRADE REACHED 5th   COLLEGE .... YEARS. OTHER OR TECHNICAL EDUCATION .... NONE   NO. YEARS SCHOOLING 7

RELIGION none CHURCH ATTENDANCE OCCASIONAL   HOW LONG SINCE LAST REGULAR ATTENDANCE? ....
NONE
EMPLOYED WHEN ARRESTED no HOW LONG .... IF UNEMPLOYED HOW LONG SINCE LAST REGULAR EMPLOYMENT 5 yrs

EMPLOYMENT RECORD — LAST THREE EMPLOYERS

EMPLOYED BY	ADDRESS	FROM	TO	NATURE OF WORK DONE	WEEKLY WAGE
Stahlmeyer Co.—127 St. N.Y.C.		7 days		Butcher	$25.00

OCCUPATION none   SKILLED
SEMI SKILLED ✓
UNSKILLED
COLLEGE TRAINED   (THESE TWO QUESTIONS TO BE DETERMINED BY INTERVIEWER FROM FOREGOING)

LAST WEEKLY WAGE $25.00 SELF SUPPORTING no SUPPORTS OTHERS AND HOW MANY

UNDER 16
MORE THAN 16
RESIDENCE WHEN ARRESTED none LENGTH OF RESIDENCE PRESENT LOCALITY .... STATE 5 yrs.

LEGAL RESIDENCE, CITY 54 4th St. N.Y.C. Pelham STATE .... COUNTRY ....

NAME AND ADDRESS OF NEAREST RELATIVE Brother Winthrop — S.A.

CRIMINAL ACTS ATTRIBUTED TO Intoxication MILITARY SERVICE. ARMY .... NAVY .... NONE ✓

PREVIOUS CRIMINAL HISTORY
(Subject To Additions And Corrections By The Bureau Of Identification)

NOTE—ADDITIONAL RECORDS AS REPORTED BY BUREAU OF CRIMINAL IDENTIFICATION TO BE ENTERED ABOVE IN RED INK.

I HEREBY CERTIFY THAT THE ABOVE IS MY CRIMINAL RECORD. I FURTHER CERTIFY THAT THE ABOVE STATEMENTS WERE MADE BY ME VOLUNTARILY AND WITHOUT ANY PROMISE OR THREAT BEING MADE AS AN INDUCEMENT TO MAKE THE SAME. I HEREBY AUTHORIZE THE WARDEN OF SING SING PRISON, OR HIS AUTHORIZED REPRESENTATIVE, TO OPEN AND EXAMINE ALL MAIL MATTER AND ALL EXPRESS AND OTHER PACKAGES WHICH MAY BE DIRECTED TO MY ADDRESS SO LONG AS I AM A PRISONER IN SAID PRISON.

THE FOLLOWING ARTICLES WERE TAKEN FROM ME WHEN I WAS RECEIVED AT SING SING PRISON, BY ....
TO BE DEPOSITED FOR ME IN THE CHIEF CLERK'S OFFICE: no property
75 $ cash

RECORD TAKEN BY .... DATE Lawrence Clinton Stone
SIGNATURE OF INMATE

123

The Worst for Last?

We are fascinated by crimes, but there is a limit to that fascination. There is a point where acts of violence are so horrific that we turn away in disgust and can't even begin to fathom the depths of depravity which compel some people to do the terrible things they do to other human beings. The hideous and revolting atrocities of Albert Fish are the ultimate examples.

While it would be remiss to exclude the story of a man who just might have been the most evil and prolific serial killer the Hudson Valley—perhaps even the entire country—has ever seen, Fish's case will not be treated in the same detailed manner as other stories in this book. The reasons for that will be immediately evident: Albert Fish tortured, mutilated, murdered, and cannibalized children. A lot of children.

FISH 'BARES' 3 MORE MURDERS, 2 UNLISTED

| Billy Gaffney | Francis McDonnell | The late Grace Budd |

In addition to murder of Grace Budd, for which he is sentenced to die, Albert H. Fish has confessed murdering the two children shown above.

Experts agree that serial killers often have a series of triggers that send them down the path of depravity, and their crimes usually continue to escalate over the course of their lives. This holds true for Fish, who said that it was the early sexual abuse and beatings he suffered at St. John's Orphanage in Washington, D.C. where it all began: "I was there 'til I was nearly nine, and that's where I got started wrong. We were unmercifully whipped. I saw boys doing many things they should not have done."

Hamilton "Albert" Fish was born in Washington, D.C. on May 19, 1870. His father was already 75 at the time, and his mother was only 32. Mental illness was prevalent in the family, with at least half a dozen close relatives being afflicted, including Albert's brother, who was confined to a mental institution, and his mother, who suffered from hallucinations. After his arrest, Albert stated that he had also been confined to the mental wards of Bellevue and Kings County Hospitals in New York, but unfortunately, he had been released each time.

At the age of five, Albert's father died and his mother did not have the resources to raise him and his three siblings, so she put the young boy in an orphanage. Four years of torment twisted his mind to the point where he actually began to enjoy the pain, violence, and sexual perversion. By the time his mother got a better job and could afford to bring him home, it was too late—the young serial killer was on his own sick path and it was only a matter of time before he began victimizing others.

He embraced both sadism and masochism. When he was 12, another boy with whom he was involved introduced him to drinking urine and eating feces. In 1890, Albert moved to New York City and became a prostitute. He also immediately began raping children, preferably very young boys. Torture soon followed, and then ultimately, murder.

While he preyed upon defenseless young boys and girls for the next 45 years, remarkably, he got married and had six children. While there is no evidence that he ever harmed his own kids, he did ask them to beat him with a paddle studded with nails. Not surprisingly, his wife left him, although why it took her so many years remains a mystery. His second marriage lasted only one week.

The details of his worst crimes are beyond our comprehension, and it is equally confounding how he got away with so many heinous acts for so long. In fact, he may never have been apprehended if it hadn't been for a letter he wrote regarding a murder he committed in a cottage behind 379 Mountain Road in Irvington, NY, on June 3, 1928.

Fish's 1903 mugshot when he was arrested for grand larceny.

Just as modern criminals now use the Internet to seek out victims, Albert Fish would scour the newspapers. In May of 1928, 18-year-old Edward Budd placed an ad in the *New York World* looking for a job. Fish went to the Budd residence, posing as a farmer under an assumed name, and offered the young man a job. Once in Fish's clutches, he intended to mutilate Edward and leave him for dead. However, his plans changed when he saw Edward's 10-year-old sister, Grace.

One of the reasons Albert Fish was able to perpetrate so many evil acts over the course of his lifetime is that he appeared to be such a mild-mannered man and he could lie so convincingly. Telling Grace's parents that he was going to his niece's birthday party and he wanted to bring Grace along, they actually allowed their daughter to accompany the stranger—and it was the last time the family would ever see her.

Albert Fish had already scouted out the cottage behind the place called the Wisteria House on Mountain Road, which at the time was in the town of Greenburgh. There he murdered Grace, cut up her body, and brought the pieces back to his apartment in New York City, where he cooked and ate them over the course of nine days. Six years later, Fish wrote letters to Grace's mother and described to her in graphic detail everything he had done to the poor girl, including saying: "How sweet and tender her little ass was roasted in the oven."

Grace Budd

Police finally had something tangible in their hands, and New York City Detective William King and his men were able to trace the source of the unique stationery on which the letter was written, and that trail led to Albert Fish. Fish confessed to murdering and eating Grace Budd, and authorities could hardly believe their ears. But it was only after they found Grace's bones buried by the cottage in Irvington that they realized just what a monster they had captured.

As if the details of his crimes against others weren't bizarre enough, the police soon learned that Fish also enjoyed harming himself. Appearing to be in some discomfort in his lower abdomen, an x-ray revealed 29 sewing needles inside of his body near his bladder! For years, Fish had been pushing the needles up through the perineum, which is the area behind the scrotum.

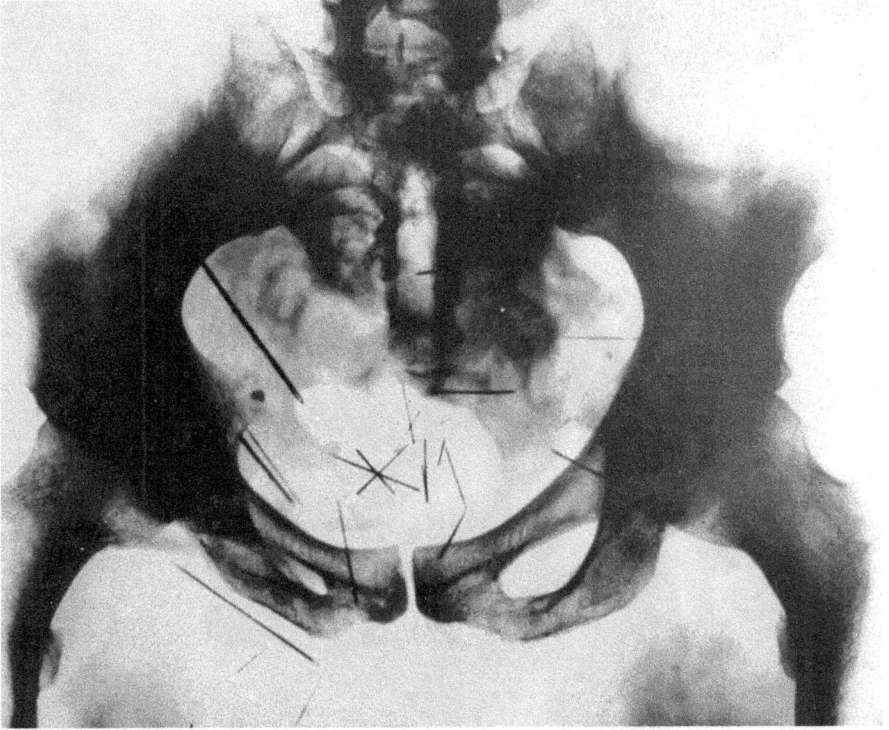

Fish also enjoyed torturing himself, as is evident by the 29 needles he thrust into his own body.

Fish confessed to a total of three murders, but claimed the real number was more like 100 victims! Dr. Frederic Wertham, a psychiatrist, also stated that after speaking with Fish he agreed that it was most likely that at least one hundred boys and girls had fallen prey to his insatiable blood lust and perversions.

The trial was a lurid affair, as shocking details of Fish's depravity and cannibalism horrified everyone in the courtroom, as well as the general public who read the startling newspaper accounts. Doctors certainly supplied enough testimony to prove that Albert Fish was about as insane as one could get, yet the verdict was still guilty. The sentence was execution by the electric chair—which completely delighted Fish. As the death sentence was being announced, the mere thought of such exquisite pain prompted him to declare that "Going to the electric chair will be the supreme thrill of my life."

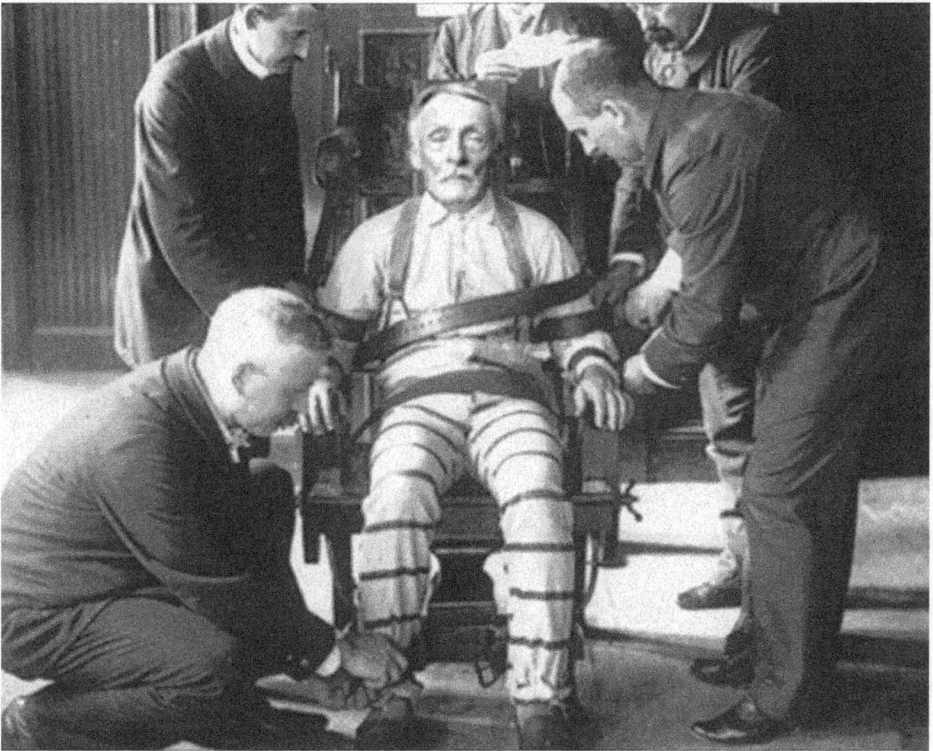

The electric chair room in Sing Sing (top) and Albert Fish being strapped in for his execution.

The guards at Sing Sing prison in Ossining probably never saw the likes of Albert Fish before, as the 65-year-old man (the oldest ever to be electrocuted in the prison) gladly helped attach the electrodes that would end his life. And Fish must have been ecstatic that the first jolt of electricity didn't do the job and that he had to be subjected to a second lethal charge. Finally, after three long minutes, he was dead.

The cottage behind Wisteria House where Fish killed Grace Budd.

Fish's biographer, Professor Harold Schechter, summed up his life:

"Albert Fish is regarded by many as the single most depraved serial killer in the annals of American crime. He practiced every known perversion found in medical texts and came up with a few of his own that no one had ever heard of."

We would like to think that in today's society we have progressed to the point where people like Albert Fish couldn't possibly get away with so many crimes over such a long period of time. But that's the most frightening thing about serial killers who are able to hide in plain sight; we don't even know that the smartest ones exist. Your neighbor, your co-worker, your child's teacher, or even your spouse could be the next murderer, and you would never know—until it's too late…

RECEIVING BLOTTER

NUMBER __90272__ NAME __Albert H. Fish__ CLASSIFICATION GROUP _____

ALIAS __Arthur Hopkins, Robert Hayden, Frank Howard, James W. Pell__

SENTENCED __3/25/35__ RECEIVED __3/25/35__ FROM __Westchester__ COUNTY.

GRADE __CC__ COLOR __W__ COURT __Supreme__ JUDGE _____

PLEA __Ver.__ CRIME __Murder, 1st degree__

TERM __Execution-Week of Apr 29, 1935__ LOST TIME _____ JAIL TIME __95__

ELIGIBLE FOR PAROLE _____

CRIMINAL ACT __Kidnapped & Killed Grace Budd-aged 10 years —__ DATE OF COMMISSION __June 3, 1928__

CITY OR TOWN WHERE CRIME WAS COMMITTED __Greenburgh, NY__

VALUE OF GOODS OR MONEY INVOLVED IN CRIME _____ RECOVERED? _____

ACCOMPLICES _____ WHERE ARE THEY NOW? _____

IS PRISONER ON FRIENDLY TERMS WITH ACCOMPLICES? _____

DATE OF BIRTH __May 19, 1870__ AGE __64__ YEARS, MENTAL AGE, _____ MENTAL DIAGNOSIS _____

NATIVITY CITY __Washington__ STATE __DC__ PORT OF ENTRY TO U. S. _____

COUNTRY _____ DATE OF ENTRY TO U. S. _____

NATIVITY OF FATHER CITY _____ STATE __Maine__ DEAD _____ NATIVITY OF MOTHER CITY _____ STATE __N.J.__ DEAD ✓

COUNTRY _____ LIVING _____ COUNTRY _____ LIVING

AGE OF PRISONER WHEN FATHER DIED __5__ WHEN MOTHER DIED __33__

NUMBER OF BROTHERS _____ SISTERS _____ SEQUENCE IN FAMILY __7th__

SINGLE _____ MARRIED __1898__ WIDOWED _____ DIVORCED _____ SEPARATED _____ COMMON LAW MARRIAGE _____ HOW LONG _____

NUMBER OF CHILDREN __6__ HABITS, MODERATE, TEMPERATE ✓ INTEMPERATE USES _____ HEALTH _____

HEIGHT _____ WEIGHT _____

EDUCATION READ ✓ WRITE ✓ ENGLISH. OTHER LANGUAGE _____ SPEAKS ENGLISH GOOD _____ AGE LEFT SCHOOL __15__

PARTIAL NONE No. YEARS SCHOOLING __8__

GRADE REACHED __8th__ COLLEGE _____ YEARS. OTHER OR TECHNICAL EDUCATION _____

RELIGION __Episcopal__ CHURCH ATTENDANCE REGULAR ✓ OCCASIONAL NONE HOW LONG SINCE LAST REGULAR ATTENDANCE? __1 week__

EMPLOYED WHEN ARRESTED __No__ HOW LONG _____ IF UNEMPLOYED HOW LONG SINCE LAST REGULAR EMPLOYMENT __2 wks—__

EMPLOYMENT RECORD — — LAST THREE EMPLOYERS

EMPLOYED BY _____ ADDRESS _____ FROM _____ TO _____ NATURE OF WORK DONE _____ WEEKLY WAGE _____

Apartment House - 336 Central Pk West - 3 weeks — Painter $30.00

OCCUPATION __Painter__ SKILLED _____ SEMI SKILLED ✓ (THESE TWO QUESTIONS TO BE DETERMINED BY INTERVIEWER FROM FOREGOING)

UNSKILLED _____ COLLEGE TRAINED _____

LAST WEEKLY WAGE __$30.00__ SELF SUPPORTING __yes__ SUPPORTS OTHERS AND HOW MANY UNDER 16 _____ MORE THAN 16 __1__

RESIDENCE WHEN ARRESTED __55 E 128 St NYC__ LENGTH OF RESIDENCE PRESENT LOCALITY _____ STATE __40 yrs—__

LEGAL RESIDENCE, CITY _____ STATE __S.A.__ COUNTRY _____

NAME AND ADDRESS OF NEAREST RELATIVE __Mrs. Gertrude O. Muno, 8-05 Astoria Blvd A_____

CRIMINAL ACTS ATTRIBUTED TO __Temporary Insanity__ MILITARY SERVICE. ARMY __No—__ NAVY __Long Island City, N.Y.__ NONE _____

PREVIOUS CRIMINAL HISTORY

(Subject To Additions And Corrections By The Bureau Of Identification)

INSTITUTION OR NAME	No.	DATE	TERM	CRIME	HOW DISCHARGED AND DATE

I HEREBY CERTIFY THAT THE ABOVE IS MY CRIMINAL RECORD. I FURTHER CERTIFY THAT THE ABOVE STATEMENTS WERE MADE BY ME VOLUNTARILY AND WITHOUT ANY PROMISE OR THREATS BEING MADE AS AN INDUCEMENT TO MAKE THE SAME. I HEREBY AUTHORIZE THE WARDEN OF SING SING PRISON, OR HIS AUTHORIZED REPRESENTATIVE, TO OPEN AND EXAMINE ALL MAIL MATTER AND ALL EXPRESS AND OTHER PACKAGES WHICH MAY BE DIRECTED TO MY ADDRESS SO LONG AS I AM A PRISONER IN SAID PRISON.

THE FOLLOWING ARTICLES WERE TAKEN FROM ME WHEN I WAS RECEIVED AT SING SING PRISON, BY _____ TO BE DEPOSITED FOR ME IN THE CHIEF CLERK'S OFFICE: __1 Wrist Watch, wallet, no cash__

RECORD TAKEN BY _____ DATE _____ SIGNATURE OF INMATE __Albert H. Fish__

Attorney: James Dempsey, Jr. Peekskill, NY

Elderly Slayer of Grace Budd Believed by the Police to Be Cannibal

All-Night Quiz Fails to Bare Other Crimes

Gives Full Details on Girl Murder—Refuses to Eat While in Cell

Continued from Page 1

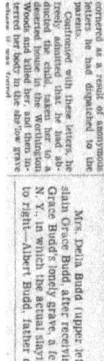

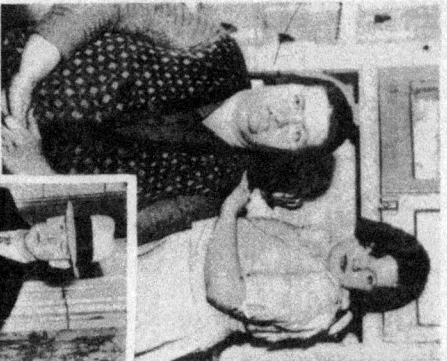

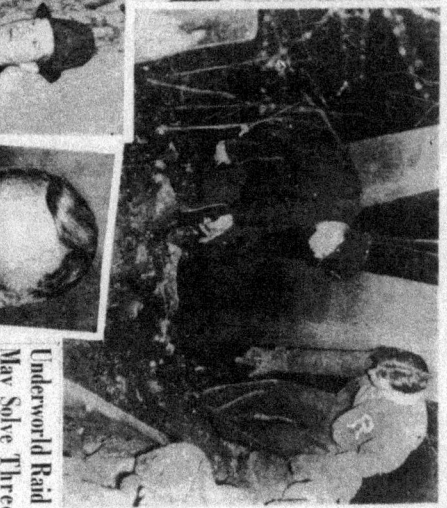

Mrs. Delia Budd (upper left) and her daughter, Beatrice, 11; mother and sister of the slain Grace Budd, after receiving news of the confession of Albert Fish. Lower right—Grace Budd's lonely grave, a few yards in the rear of an abandoned house in Elmsford, N. Y., in which the actual slaying is believed to have taken place. Upper right, left to right—Albert H. Fish, father of Grace; Edward Budd, the slain girl's brother; and Fish.

I'll See He Gets His, Girl's Brother Says

Family Tells How Fish Flattered His Money and How Impressed They Were by His $10 Hat—Trusted Him Implicitly

Underworld Raid May Solve Three Crimes, Police Say

4 Men and Woman Arrested in Arsenal-To-Drag Delaware for Weiss' Body

Traffic Case Against Judge

Please visit the author's
website at:
www.gotozim.com

www.ingramcontent.com/pod-product-compliance
Lightning Source LLC
Chambersburg PA
CBHW030020290326
41934CB00005B/417